HowExpert to Stone Skipping

A Comprehensive Manual on How to Stone Skip, Master Stone Skipping Techniques, Excel in Competitions, and Connect with the Stone Skipping Community

HowExpert

Copyright © Hot Methods, Inc. DBA HowExpert™
www.HowExpert.com

For more tips related to this topic, visit HowExpert.com/stoneskipping.

Recommended Resources

- HowExpert.com – How To Guides on All Topics from A to Z by Everyday Experts.
- HowExpert.com/free – Free HowExpert Email Newsletter.
- HowExpert.com/books – HowExpert Books
- HowExpert.com/courses – HowExpert Courses
- HowExpert.com/clothing – HowExpert Clothing
- HowExpert.com/membership – HowExpert Membership Site
- HowExpert.com/affiliates – HowExpert Affiliate Program
- HowExpert.com/jobs – HowExpert Jobs
- HowExpert.com/writers – Write About Your #1 Passion/Knowledge/Expertise & Become a HowExpert Author.
- HowExpert.com/resources – Additional HowExpert Recommended Resources
- YouTube.com/HowExpert – Subscribe to HowExpert YouTube.
- Instagram.com/HowExpert – Follow HowExpert on Instagram.
- Facebook.com/HowExpert – Follow HowExpert on Facebook.
- TikTok.com/@HowExpert – Follow HowExpert on TikTok.

Publisher's Foreword

Dear HowExpert Reader,

HowExpert publishes quick 'how to' guides on all topics from A to Z by everyday experts.

At HowExpert, our mission is to discover, empower, and maximize everyday people's talents to ultimately make a positive impact in the world for all topics from A to Z...one everyday expert at a time!

HowExpert guides are written by everyday people just like you and me, who have a passion, knowledge, and expertise for a specific topic.

We take great pride in selecting everyday experts who have a passion, real-life experience in a topic, and excellent writing skills to teach you about the topic you are also passionate about and eager to learn.

We hope you get a lot of value from our HowExpert guides, and it can make a positive impact on your life in some way. All of our readers, including you, help us continue living our mission of positively impacting the world for all spheres of influences from A to Z.

If you enjoyed one of our HowExpert guides, then please take a moment to send us your feedback from wherever you got this book.

Thank you, and I wish you all the best in all aspects of life.

To your success,

Byungjoon "BJ" Min / 민병준
Founder & Publisher of HowExpert
HowExpert.com

PS...If you are also interested in becoming a HowExpert author, then please visit our website at HowExpert.com/writers. Thank you & again, all the best! John 3:16

COPYRIGHT, LEGAL NOTICE AND DISCLAIMER:

COPYRIGHT © HOT METHODS, INC. (DBA HOWEXPERT™). ALL RIGHTS RESERVED WORLDWIDE. NO PART OF THIS PUBLICATION MAY BE REPRODUCED IN ANY FORM OR BY ANY MEANS, INCLUDING SCANNING, PHOTOCOPYING, OR OTHERWISE WITHOUT PRIOR WRITTEN PERMISSION OF THE COPYRIGHT HOLDER.

DISCLAIMER AND TERMS OF USE: PLEASE NOTE THAT MUCH OF THIS PUBLICATION IS BASED ON PERSONAL EXPERIENCE AND ANECDOTAL EVIDENCE. ALTHOUGH THE AUTHOR AND PUBLISHER HAVE MADE EVERY REASONABLE ATTEMPT TO ACHIEVE COMPLETE ACCURACY OF THE CONTENT IN THIS GUIDE, THEY ASSUME NO RESPONSIBILITY FOR ERRORS OR OMISSIONS. ALSO, YOU SHOULD USE THIS INFORMATION AS YOU SEE FIT, AND AT YOUR OWN RISK. YOUR PARTICULAR SITUATION MAY NOT BE EXACTLY SUITED TO THE EXAMPLES ILLUSTRATED HERE; IN FACT, IT'S LIKELY THAT THEY WON'T BE THE SAME, AND YOU SHOULD ADJUST YOUR USE OF THE INFORMATION AND RECOMMENDATIONS ACCORDINGLY.

THE AUTHOR AND PUBLISHER DO NOT WARRANT THE PERFORMANCE, EFFECTIVENESS OR APPLICABILITY OF ANY SITES LISTED OR LINKED TO IN THIS BOOK. ALL LINKS ARE FOR INFORMATION PURPOSES ONLY AND ARE NOT WARRANTED FOR CONTENT, ACCURACY OR ANY OTHER IMPLIED OR EXPLICIT PURPOSE.

ANY TRADEMARKS, SERVICE MARKS, PRODUCT NAMES OR NAMED FEATURES ARE ASSUMED TO BE THE PROPERTY OF THEIR RESPECTIVE OWNERS, AND ARE USED ONLY FOR REFERENCE. THERE IS NO IMPLIED ENDORSEMENT IF WE USE ONE OF THESE TERMS.

NO PART OF THIS BOOK MAY BE REPRODUCED, STORED IN A RETRIEVAL SYSTEM, OR TRANSMITTED BY ANY OTHER MEANS: ELECTRONIC, MECHANICAL, PHOTOCOPYING, RECORDING, OR OTHERWISE, WITHOUT THE PRIOR WRITTEN PERMISSION OF THE AUTHOR.

ANY VIOLATION BY STEALING THIS BOOK OR DOWNLOADING OR SHARING IT ILLEGALLY WILL BE PROSECUTED BY LAWYERS TO THE FULLEST EXTENT. THIS PUBLICATION IS PROTECTED UNDER THE US COPYRIGHT ACT OF 1976 AND ALL OTHER APPLICABLE INTERNATIONAL, FEDERAL, STATE AND LOCAL LAWS AND ALL RIGHTS ARE RESERVED, INCLUDING RESALE RIGHTS: YOU ARE NOT ALLOWED TO GIVE OR SELL THIS GUIDE TO ANYONE ELSE.

THIS PUBLICATION IS DESIGNED TO PROVIDE ACCURATE AND AUTHORITATIVE INFORMATION WITH REGARD TO THE SUBJECT MATTER COVERED. IT IS SOLD WITH THE UNDERSTANDING THAT THE AUTHORS AND PUBLISHERS ARE NOT ENGAGED IN RENDERING LEGAL, FINANCIAL, OR OTHER PROFESSIONAL ADVICE. LAWS AND PRACTICES OFTEN VARY FROM STATE TO STATE AND IF LEGAL OR OTHER EXPERT ASSISTANCE IS REQUIRED, THE SERVICES OF A PROFESSIONAL SHOULD BE SOUGHT. THE AUTHORS AND PUBLISHER SPECIFICALLY DISCLAIM ANY LIABILITY THAT IS INCURRED FROM THE USE OR APPLICATION OF THE CONTENTS OF THIS BOOK.

HOT METHODS, INC. DBA HOWEXPERT
EMAIL: SUPPORT@HOWEXPERT.COM
WEBSITE: WWW.HOWEXPERT.COM

**COPYRIGHT © HOT METHODS, INC. (DBA HOWEXPERT™)
ALL RIGHTS RESERVED WORLDWIDE.**

Table of Contents

Recommended Resources 2
Publisher's Foreword 3
Book Overview 10
Introduction 14
   Welcome to the World of Stone Skipping 14
      The Joy and Art of Stone Skipping 14
   Benefits of Stone Skipping 15
      1. Physical Benefits: 15
      2. Mental Benefits: 15
      3. Social Benefits: 15
   How to Use This Guide 16
Chapter 1: History and Culture of Stone Skipping 17
   1.1 The Origins of Stone Skipping 17
      1.1.1 Ancient Beginnings 17
      1.1.2 Evolution Over the Centuries 18
      Conclusion of Section 1.1 20
   1.2 Stone Skipping Around the World 20
      1.2.1 Cultural Variations 21
      1.2.2 Notable Stone Skipping Locations 23
      Conclusion of Section 1.2 25
   1.3 Famous Stone Skippers and Records 25
      1.3.1 Legendary Skippers 26
      1.3.2 World Records and Competitions 27
   Chapter 1 Review 29
Chapter 2: Understanding the Science of Stone Skipping 32

2.1 The Physics of Stone Skipping 32
    2.1.1 Basic Principles of Physics 32
    2.1.2 Forces Involved in Stone Skipping 34
2.2 The Ideal Angle and Speed 35
    2.2.1 Optimal Angles for Skipping 36
    2.2.2 Speed and Spin Dynamics 37
2.3 Hydrodynamics 39
    2.3.1 Interaction Between Stone and Water 39
    2.3.2 Impact of Water Surface Tension 41
Chapter 2 Review 43

Chapter 3: Selecting the Perfect Stone 45
3.1 Types of Stones 45
    3.1.1 Flat Stones vs. Rounded Stones 45
    3.1.2 Best Stones for Skipping 46
3.2 Finding Stones in Nature 48
    3.2.1 Ideal Locations for Stone Hunting 48
    3.2.2 Tips for Spotting Good Skipping Stones 50
3.3 Preparing Your Stones 52
    3.3.1 Cleaning and Shaping 52
    3.3.2 Storing Your Stones 54
Chapter 3 Review: Selecting the Perfect Stone 55

Chapter 4: Techniques for Skipping Stones 57
4.1 Basic Stone Skipping Technique 57
    4.1.1 Proper Grip and Stance 57
    4.1.2 Wind-Up and Release 59
4.2 Advanced Skipping Techniques 61
    4.2.1 Increasing Spin and Speed 61

4.2.2 Mastering the Skip Count 63
4.3 Common Mistakes and How to Avoid Them 64
4.3.1 Identifying Errors 65
4.3.2 Tips for Consistent Skipping 67
Chapter 4 Review: Techniques for Skipping Stones 69

Chapter 5: Practicing and Perfecting Your Skills 71
5.1 Setting Up Practice Sessions 71
5.1.1 Finding the Right Practice Spot 71
5.1.2 Optimal Conditions for Practice 73
5.2 Drills and Exercises 75
5.2.1 Improving Technique and Form 75
5.2.2 Building Strength and Precision 78
5.3 Tracking Your Progress 81
5.3.1 Keeping a Skipping Log 82
5.3.2 Analyzing Your Performance 83
Chapter 5 Review: Practicing and Perfecting Your Skills 85

Chapter 6: Competing in Stone Skipping 88
6.1 Local and National Competitions 88
6.1.1 Finding Competitions Near You 88
6.1.2 Preparing for Your First Competition 90
6.2 Rules and Regulations 92
6.2.1 Understanding Competition Rules 93
6.2.2 Fair Play and Sportsmanship 95
6.3 Strategies for Winning 97
6.3.1 Mental Preparation 97
6.3.2 Competitive Techniques 99
Chapter 6 Review: Competing in Stone Skipping 102

Chapter 7: The Community of Stone Skipping 105

7.1 Connecting with Fellow Enthusiasts 105

7.1.1 Joining Clubs and Groups 105

7.1.2 Online Communities and Forums 107

7.2 Events and Gatherings 109

7.2.1 Attending Stone Skipping Festivals 109

7.2.2 Hosting Your Own Skipping Event 111

7.3 Promoting the Sport 114

7.3.1 Teaching Others 114

7.3.2 Advocacy and Conservation 116

Chapter 7 Review: The Community of Stone Skipping 118

Chapter 8: Stone Skipping for All Ages 122

8.1 Teaching Kids to Skip Stones 122

8.1.1 Simplified Techniques for Children 122

8.1.2 Safety Tips for Young Skippers 124

8.2 Stone Skipping as a Family Activity 127

8.2.1 Fun Games and Challenges 127

8.2.2 Building Family Traditions 130

8.3 Stone Skipping for Seniors 133

8.3.1 Adjusting Techniques for Older Adults 134

8.3.2 Benefits of Stone Skipping for Seniors 136

Chapter 8 Review: Stone Skipping for All Ages 138

Chapter 9: Conclusion 142

9.1 Reflecting on Your Stone Skipping Journey 142

9.1.1 Celebrating Your Progress 142

9.1.2 Setting Future Goals 144

9.2 Staying Engaged with Stone Skipping 146

- 9.2.1 Continual Learning and Improvement 146
- 9.2.2 Exploring New Locations 148
- 9.3 The Legacy of Stone Skipping 149
  - 9.3.1 Passing Down the Tradition 150
  - 9.3.2 Inspiring Future Generations 151
- Chapter 9 Review: Conclusion 153
- Chapter 10: Appendix 156
  - 10.1 Resources and References 156
    - 10.1.1 Books and Articles 156
    - 10.1.2 Websites and Online Resources 159
  - 10.2 Glossary of Stone Skipping Terms 162
    - 10.2.1 Key Terminology Explained 162
  - 10.3 Frequently Asked Questions 166
    - 10.3.1 Common Queries and Answers 166
- About the Author 171
- About the Publisher 172
- Recommended Resources 173

Book Overview

If you've ever been fascinated by the magic of a perfectly skipped stone, then HowExpert Guide to Stone Skipping is your ultimate resource. This comprehensive guide is your companion to mastering the timeless art of stone skipping, packed with insights, techniques, and tips for skippers of all levels.

What This Guide Offers:

Introduction

- Welcome to the World of Stone Skipping: Discover the joy and art of stone skipping, its benefits, and how to make the most of this guide.

Chapter 1: History and Culture of Stone Skipping

- The Origins of Stone Skipping: Explore the ancient beginnings and evolution of stone skipping over the centuries.

- Stone Skipping Around the World: Learn about cultural variations and notable stone skipping locations worldwide.

- Famous Stone Skippers and Records: Discover legendary skippers, world records, and major competitions.

Chapter 2: Understanding the Science of Stone Skipping

- The Physics of Stone Skipping: Understand the basic principles of physics and the forces involved in stone skipping.

- The Ideal Angle and Speed: Learn about optimal angles for skipping, and the dynamics of speed and spin.

- Hydrodynamics: Discover the interaction between the stone and water, and the impact of water surface tension.

Chapter 3: Selecting the Perfect Stone

- Types of Stones: Differentiate between flat and rounded stones, and identify the best stones for skipping.

- Finding Stones in Nature: Find out where to hunt for ideal skipping stones and how to spot them in natural settings.

- Preparing Your Stones: Learn how to clean, shape, and store your stones for optimal performance.

Chapter 4: Techniques for Skipping Stones

- Basic Stone Skipping Technique: Master the proper grip, stance, wind-up, and release for successful skips.

- Advanced Skipping Techniques: Improve your skills with techniques to increase spin, speed, and skip count.

- Common Mistakes and How to Avoid Them: Identify common errors and get tips for consistent skipping.

Chapter 5: Practicing and Perfecting Your Skills

- Setting Up Practice Sessions: Learn how to find the right practice spots and optimal conditions for practice.

- Drills and Exercises: Engage in drills to improve your technique and build strength and precision.

- Tracking Your Progress: Keep a skipping log and analyze your performance for continual improvement.

Chapter 6: Competing in Stone Skipping

- Local and National Competitions: Discover how to find competitions, prepare for your first event, and understand the rules.

- Strategies for Winning: Learn mental preparation and competitive techniques to excel in stone skipping contests.

Chapter 7: The Community of Stone Skipping

- Connecting with Fellow Enthusiasts: Join clubs, online communities, and participate in events and gatherings.

- Promoting the Sport: Teach others, advocate for the sport, and engage in conservation efforts.

Chapter 8: Stone Skipping for All Ages

- Teaching Kids to Skip Stones: Learn simplified techniques and safety tips for young skippers.

- Stone Skipping as a Family Activity: Enjoy fun games and challenges, and build family traditions.

- Stone Skipping for Seniors: Adjust techniques for older adults and discover the benefits of stone skipping for seniors.

Chapter 9: Conclusion

- Reflecting on Your Stone Skipping Journey: Celebrate your progress, set future goals, and stay engaged with the sport.

- The Legacy of Stone Skipping: Pass down the tradition and inspire future generations.

Appendix

- Resources and References: Access a wealth of books, articles, and online resources.

- Glossary of Stone Skipping Terms: Understand key terminology.

- Frequently Asked Questions: Find answers to common queries.

If you want to master the art of stone skipping and join a community of passionate skippers, then HowExpert Guide to Stone Skipping is your ultimate resource. This comprehensive guide provides you with the knowledge, techniques, and inspiration to become a stone skipping master.

Read your copy today and start your journey to stone skipping excellence!

HowExpert publishes how to guides on all topics from A to Z. Visit HowExpert.com to learn more.

Introduction

Welcome to the World of Stone Skipping

Stone skipping is more than just a pastime; it's an art, a science, and a cherished tradition that transcends generations. This guide is designed to take you on a journey through the fascinating world of stone skipping, offering you the knowledge and techniques needed to master this delightful activity. Whether you are a beginner looking to learn the basics or an experienced skipper aiming to perfect your skills, this guide will provide you with everything you need to know about stone skipping.

The Joy and Art of Stone Skipping

Stone skipping is a simple yet captivating activity that brings joy to people of all ages. The thrill of watching a stone gracefully bounce across the water's surface, leaving behind ripples of excitement, is a feeling like no other.

1. A Connection with Nature: Stone skipping allows you to interact with nature in a unique and peaceful way. The search for the perfect stone, the feel of the cool water, and the serene environment all contribute to a deeply satisfying experience.
2. A Creative Expression: Each stone skip is a unique creation, a blend of technique, timing, and personal flair. The way you choose and throw your stone reflects your individual style and creativity.
3. A Source of Challenge and Achievement: Mastering the art of stone skipping requires practice and precision. Achieving a perfect skip or setting a new personal record offers a sense of accomplishment and pride.

Benefits of Stone Skipping

Engaging in stone skipping offers numerous benefits beyond the immediate pleasure of the activity itself. These benefits span physical, mental, and social aspects, making stone skipping a well-rounded and enriching hobby.

1. Physical Benefits:

   - Improved Hand-Eye Coordination: The process of aiming and throwing stones enhances your hand-eye coordination and fine motor skills.

   - Increased Physical Activity: Searching for stones, bending, throwing, and walking along the shore contribute to a moderate level of physical exercise.

2. Mental Benefits:

   - Stress Relief: The rhythmic and repetitive nature of stone skipping can be meditative, helping to reduce stress and promote relaxation.

   - Enhanced Focus and Patience: Achieving the perfect skip requires concentration and patience, skills that are beneficial in many areas of life.

3. Social Benefits:

   - Community and Bonding: Stone skipping is a social activity that can bring people together. Whether it's a friendly competition or a leisurely day at the lake with family and friends, it fosters connections and shared experiences.

   - Educational Value: Teaching children or newcomers the art of stone skipping can be a rewarding experience, passing down knowledge and tradition.

How to Use This Guide

This guide is structured to provide you with a comprehensive understanding of stone skipping, from its history and cultural significance to the practical techniques and strategies required to become an adept stone skipper. Here's how you can make the most out of this guide:

1. Sequential Learning: The chapters are organized in a systematic and sequenced manner, starting with the basics and gradually progressing to more advanced topics. Follow the chapters in order for a structured learning experience.
2. Practical Application: Each chapter includes practical tips, exercises, and drills that you can apply immediately. Practice regularly to improve your skills and track your progress.
3. Deep Dive Sections: For those interested in exploring specific aspects of stone skipping in greater detail, deep dive sections are provided. These sections offer in-depth insights into the science, history, and advanced techniques of stone skipping.
4. Interactive Elements: Engage with the guide actively by participating in suggested activities, joining stone skipping communities, and attending events or competitions mentioned in the guide.
5. Resourceful Appendices: The appendices provide additional resources, including books, articles, online communities, and a glossary of terms to enhance your understanding and keep you connected with the stone skipping community.

By the end of this guide, you will have acquired the skills, knowledge, and confidence to enjoy and excel in the art of stone skipping. So, grab your stones, find a calm body of water, and let's embark on this exciting journey together!

Chapter 1: History and Culture of Stone Skipping

Stone skipping is more than just a simple pastime; it has a rich history and cultural significance that spans the globe. This chapter explores the origins, evolution, and global variations of stone skipping, as well as highlighting notable skippers and record-breaking feats.

1.1 The Origins of Stone Skipping

Stone skipping, also known as stone skimming, is a pastime that has fascinated people across the globe for centuries. The simplicity of throwing a stone across the water's surface and watching it skip elegantly is a universal delight that transcends cultures and generations. This chapter delves into the rich history and cultural significance of stone skipping, tracing its roots from ancient times to its evolution over the centuries.

1.1.1 Ancient Beginnings

The art of stone skipping dates back to ancient times when early humans found joy in the simple act of throwing flat stones across water. Evidence suggests that stone skipping was practiced by various ancient civilizations, each contributing to the tradition in unique ways.

A. Early Evidence and Archaeological Finds

- Archaeological discoveries have unearthed ancient tools and carvings that depict scenes of stone skipping. These artifacts indicate that stone skipping was not only a recreational activity but also a form of early human expression and enjoyment.

- In some ancient cultures, flat stones were specifically shaped and used for skipping, suggesting a deliberate and sophisticated approach to the activity.

B. Mythology and Folklore

- Many ancient myths and legends feature gods, heroes, and mythical creatures engaging in stone skipping. In Greek mythology, for instance, it was believed that the gods would skip stones across the seas as a playful pastime.

- Folktales from various cultures often include stories of skillful stone skippers who could perform incredible feats, such as making a stone skip a dozen times or more, impressing onlookers with their prowess.

C. Practical Uses and Symbolism

- Beyond recreation, stone skipping may have served practical purposes in ancient societies. It is speculated that early humans used the activity to hone their hunting and throwing skills, which were crucial for survival.

- Symbolically, the act of making a stone skip across water could represent various themes, such as overcoming obstacles, achieving harmony with nature, and demonstrating physical and mental prowess.

1.1.2 Evolution Over the Centuries

As civilizations evolved, so did the practice of stone skipping. The activity transformed from a simple pastime to a more structured and recognized form of recreation, gaining popularity and significance over time.

A. Middle Ages and Renaissance

- During the Middle Ages, stone skipping continued to be a popular activity among children and adults alike. It was often enjoyed during leisurely walks by lakes and rivers, providing a moment of relaxation and entertainment.

- The Renaissance period saw a resurgence of interest in natural sciences and outdoor activities. Stone skipping became a subject of curiosity, with scholars and artists depicting the activity in their works, celebrating its simplicity and beauty.

B. Modern Era and Competitive Skipping

- The late 19th and early 20th centuries marked the beginning of organized stone skipping competitions. Enthusiasts began to gather for friendly contests, measuring the number of skips and the distance achieved by each throw.

- In 1903, the first recorded stone skipping competition took place in Scotland, setting the stage for the formalization of rules and the recognition of stone skipping as a legitimate sport.

C. Global Spread and Cultural Impact

- Stone skipping gained international popularity, with various countries adopting the activity and adding their unique twists. In Japan, for example, stone skipping is known as "mizu-kiri" and is considered both a sport and an art form.

- The late 20th century saw the formation of stone skipping associations and clubs around the world. These organizations played a crucial role in promoting the activity, organizing competitions, and preserving the cultural heritage of stone skipping.

D. Technological Advances and Media Exposure

- The advent of the internet and social media has greatly contributed to the global spread of stone skipping. Videos showcasing impressive skips and tutorials have captivated audiences, inspiring new generations of skippers.

- Television programs and documentaries have featured stone skipping, highlighting its history, cultural significance, and the skill involved. This media exposure has brought stone skipping into the mainstream, attracting more participants and enthusiasts.

Conclusion of Section 1.1

The origins and evolution of stone skipping are a testament to the enduring appeal of this simple yet captivating activity. From ancient beginnings to modern-day competitions, stone skipping has woven itself into the fabric of human culture, symbolizing creativity, skill, and a deep connection with nature. As we continue to explore the art and science of stone skipping, understanding its rich history enriches our appreciation and inspires us to carry forward this timeless tradition.

1.2 Stone Skipping Around the World

Stone skipping is a beloved pastime that transcends borders and cultures, reflecting the universal appeal of making stones dance across the water's surface. This section explores how different cultures have embraced stone skipping, highlighting unique traditions, techniques, and the most iconic locations around the globe where stone skipping is celebrated.

1.2.1 Cultural Variations

Stone skipping has been adopted and adapted by various cultures, each bringing its unique flair to the activity. These cultural variations reveal the diverse ways in which people around the world engage with this simple yet captivating pastime.

A. Japan: Mizu-Kiri

- Mizu-Kiri (water-cutting) is the Japanese art of stone skipping. It emphasizes precision and grace, reflecting the Japanese appreciation for beauty and skill.

- Traditional Mizu-Kiri involves specific techniques for selecting stones and throwing them, often practiced in serene natural settings such as lakes and calm rivers.

- In Japan, stone skipping is sometimes included in local festivals, and there are even competitions where participants are judged on both the number of skips and the aesthetic quality of their throws.

B. United States: Competitive Stone Skipping

- The United States has a rich tradition of competitive stone skipping, with organized events held annually in various states.

- The National Stone Skipping Competition on Mackinac Island, Michigan, is one of the most renowned, attracting participants from across the country.

- In American competitions, the focus is often on the number of skips and the distance achieved, with official rules and regulations to ensure fairness.

C. Scotland: Skimming Stones

- Scotland, known for its rugged coastlines and numerous lochs, has a long history of stone skimming.

- Stone skimming in Scotland is often a family activity, enjoyed during outings by the water.

- The Scottish Open Stone Skimming Championships, held on Easdale Island, is a major event that draws skippers from around the world, emphasizing both the number of skips and the distance covered.

D. United Kingdom: The Art of Stone Skimming

- In the UK, stone skimming is a cherished tradition often passed down through generations.

- The British Stone Skimming Championships, held in Wales, is a highlight of the stone skimming calendar, featuring both serious competitors and enthusiastic amateurs.

- The UK also boasts beautiful natural spots ideal for stone skimming, such as the Lake District and the coastal areas of Cornwall.

E. Other Notable Cultures

- Australia: In Australia, stone skipping is a popular beach activity, with children and adults alike enjoying the challenge of achieving the perfect skip.

- France: Along the rivers and lakes of France, stone skipping is a leisurely activity often accompanied by picnics and outdoor gatherings.

- India: In rural parts of India, stone skipping is a common pastime among children, who often compete to see who can achieve the most skips with a single throw.

1.2.2 Notable Stone Skipping Locations

The world is full of picturesque locations that are perfect for stone skipping. These notable spots offer not only ideal conditions for the activity but also stunning natural beauty that enhances the overall experience.

A. Mackinac Island, Michigan, USA

- Home to the National Stone Skipping Competition, Mackinac Island offers ideal stone skipping conditions with its calm waters and abundant flat stones.

- The island's scenic beauty, with its historic buildings and lush greenery, provides a perfect backdrop for stone skipping enthusiasts.

B. Easdale Island, Scotland

- Easdale Island hosts the Scottish Open Stone Skimming Championships, held in a disused quarry filled with water.

- The unique location, with its dramatic landscapes and tranquil waters, makes it a prime destination for stone skippers.

C. Lake Biwa, Japan

- Lake Biwa, Japan's largest freshwater lake, is a popular spot for Mizu-Kiri enthusiasts.

- The clear, calm waters of Lake Biwa, surrounded by picturesque mountains, create an ideal setting for practicing the art of stone skipping.

D. Lake District, United Kingdom

- The Lake District's numerous lakes and scenic beauty make it a favorite destination for stone skippers.

- Locations such as Windermere and Derwentwater offer excellent conditions for skipping stones, with plenty of flat stones and peaceful waters.

E. Bondi Beach, Australia

- Bondi Beach, famous for its stunning coastline, provides ample opportunities for stone skipping along its sandy shores.

- The beach's vibrant atmosphere and beautiful views make it a popular spot for locals and tourists alike.

F. Loire Valley, France

- The Loire Valley, with its meandering rivers and charming landscapes, is an excellent location for stone skipping.

- The region's serene environment and picturesque settings add to the enjoyment of the activity.

G. Kerala Backwaters, India

- The tranquil backwaters of Kerala offer perfect conditions for stone skipping, with their calm, reflective waters.

- The lush greenery and peaceful ambiance of the backwaters make stone skipping a relaxing and enjoyable experience.

Conclusion of Section 1.2

Stone skipping is a universal activity that brings joy and connection to people across the globe. By exploring the cultural variations and notable locations for stone skipping, we gain a deeper appreciation for how this simple pastime has been embraced and celebrated in diverse ways. Whether you are practicing Mizu-Kiri in Japan or competing in the National Stone Skipping Competition in the USA, the essence of stone skipping remains the same – a harmonious blend of skill, nature, and pure enjoyment. As you continue your journey in mastering stone skipping, take inspiration from these global traditions and iconic locations, adding your unique touch to this timeless activity.

1.3 Famous Stone Skippers and Records

Stone skipping is not just a casual pastime; it has a rich history of legendary skippers and impressive records that have captured the imagination of enthusiasts worldwide. This section delves into the stories of these remarkable individuals and the records they have set, providing inspiration and benchmarks for aspiring stone skippers.

1.3.1 Legendary Skippers

Throughout the history of stone skipping, several individuals have distinguished themselves with their exceptional skill and dedication to the art. These legendary skippers have set the standards and inspired countless others to pursue the perfect skip.

A. Kurt Steiner: The King of Skipping

- Background: Kurt Steiner, often referred to as "Mountain Man," is a name synonymous with stone skipping excellence. Hailing from the United States, Steiner has dedicated much of his life to mastering the art of stone skipping.

- Achievements: Steiner holds multiple world records in stone skipping, including the current Guinness World Record for the most skips on a single throw. His record-setting throw achieved an astonishing 88 skips.

- Techniques: Steiner's success can be attributed to his meticulous approach to selecting and preparing stones, as well as his precise throwing technique. He often emphasizes the importance of patience, practice, and understanding the physics behind each throw.

B. Russell Byars: The Competitive Spirit

- Background: Russell "Rock Bottom" Byars, another prominent figure in the world of stone skipping, hails from Pennsylvania, USA. Byars has competed in numerous stone skipping competitions and is known for his competitive spirit and technical prowess.

- Achievements: Byars previously held the Guinness World Record for the most skips, with a throw that achieved 51 skips. His record stood until Kurt Steiner surpassed it.

- Techniques: Byars is known for his powerful throws and ability to achieve a high number of skips even in less-than-ideal conditions. His technique involves a strong, consistent spin and a low-angle release.

C. Max Steiner: The Young Prodigy

- Background: Max Steiner, the son of Kurt Steiner, has quickly made a name for himself in the stone skipping community. Despite his young age, Max has demonstrated exceptional skill and a deep understanding of the art.

- Achievements: Max has participated in several competitions and often competes alongside his father. His technique and dedication have earned him recognition as a rising star in the sport.

- Techniques: Max's technique is influenced by his father's teachings but also incorporates his unique style, characterized by precise control and smooth, consistent throws.

D. Other Notable Skippers

- Rick Reaser: Known for his consistent performance in competitions and his innovative skipping techniques.

- John "Skipper" Kiefer: A veteran in the stone skipping community, celebrated for his long-standing contributions and mentoring of younger skippers.

1.3.2 World Records and Competitions

The world of stone skipping is not just about personal achievement; it is also about pushing the boundaries of what is possible. Competitions and records play a crucial role in this endeavor, providing skippers with goals to strive for and a platform to showcase their skills.

A. Guinness World Records

- Most Skips: The Guinness World Record for the most skips currently stands at 88 skips, set by Kurt Steiner in 2013. This record represents the pinnacle of stone skipping achievement.

- Other Records: In addition to the most skips, records are also recognized for the longest distance achieved with a single skip and the highest number of skips in a limited time frame.

B. National Stone Skipping Competitions

- USA: The National Stone Skipping Competition held annually on Mackinac Island, Michigan, is one of the most prestigious events in the stone skipping calendar. It attracts top skippers from across the country and features various categories and age groups.

- Scotland: The Scottish Open Stone Skimming Championships, held on Easdale Island, is another major event. Competitors from around the world gather to showcase their skills in a picturesque setting.

C. International Competitions

- Japan: Japan hosts several stone skipping events, with Mizu-Kiri competitions being particularly popular. These events emphasize both technical skill and aesthetic appeal.

- Global Competitions: Stone skipping competitions are held in various countries, each with its unique rules and traditions. These events foster a sense of global community among stone skippers.

D. Judging Criteria and Rules

- Number of Skips: Competitions typically judge throws based on the number of skips achieved. A skip is defined as each contact the stone makes with the water's surface.

- Distance: Some competitions also measure the distance covered by the stone after it stops skipping. This requires a combination of power and control.

- Technique: Judges may also consider the throw's technique, including the stone's spin, the angle of release, and the skipper's form.

- Fair Play: Adherence to competition rules and sportsmanship is crucial. Skippers must use stones provided by the organizers to ensure fairness.

Conclusion of Section 1.3

The stories of legendary skippers and the impressive records they have set highlight the extraordinary skill and dedication required to excel in stone skipping. Competitions around the world provide a platform for skippers to showcase their talents and push the limits of what is possible. By studying these examples and participating in competitions, aspiring stone skippers can draw inspiration and set their own goals for achievement in this timeless and universally beloved activity.

Chapter 1 Review

In Chapter 1: History and Culture of Stone Skipping, the focus is on the rich history, cultural significance, and notable figures in the world of stone skipping. Here's a detailed review of each section:

- 1.1 The Origins of Stone Skipping

- Ancient Beginnings: This section explores the early history of stone skipping, tracing its origins back to ancient civilizations. It highlights how early humans discovered the joy and challenge of making stones skip across water.

- Evolution Over the Centuries: Learn how stone skipping evolved over time, becoming a popular pastime in various cultures. This part covers significant milestones in the development of stone skipping techniques and traditions.

- 1.2 Stone Skipping Around the World

- Cultural Variations: Discover how stone skipping is practiced differently across cultures. This section delves into regional variations, unique techniques, and the cultural importance of stone skipping in different parts of the world.

- Notable Stone Skipping Locations: Explore famous locations known for stone skipping. These spots are celebrated for their ideal conditions and have become popular destinations for enthusiasts.

- 1.3 Famous Stone Skippers and Records

- Legendary Skippers: Learn about the legendary figures in the world of stone skipping. This section highlights the achievements and contributions of famous skippers who have left a mark on the sport.

- World Records and Competitions: Get insights into the world records and notable competitions in stone skipping. This part covers the most impressive records, the history of competitive stone skipping, and major events where the best skippers showcase their skills.

Summary

Chapter 1 provides a comprehensive overview of the history and culture of stone skipping. By exploring its ancient origins and evolution, you gain an appreciation for the pastime's long-standing appeal. The chapter highlights the cultural variations and notable locations around the world, showcasing the global reach of stone skipping. Additionally, learning about famous skippers and world records adds a sense of achievement and excitement to the sport. This chapter sets the stage for understanding the broader context of stone skipping and its significance throughout history.

Chapter 2: Understanding the Science of Stone Skipping

Mastering the art of stone skipping is not just about practice and technique; it's also about understanding the science behind it. This chapter delves into the physics and hydrodynamics of stone skipping, providing you with the foundational knowledge needed to elevate your stone skipping game.

2.1 The Physics of Stone Skipping

Mastering stone skipping involves more than just technique and practice; it requires an understanding of the underlying physics that make it possible. This section explores the basic principles of physics and the specific forces involved in stone skipping, providing a scientific foundation for improving your skills.

2.1.1 Basic Principles of Physics

Understanding the basic principles of physics is essential for grasping how stone skipping works. Here are the fundamental concepts:

A. Newton's First Law of Motion (Inertia)

- Principle: An object in motion stays in motion with the same speed and direction unless acted upon by an unbalanced external force.

- Application: When you throw a stone, it will continue to move forward in a straight line until forces like gravity, water resistance, and friction cause it to slow down and eventually stop.

B. Newton's Second Law of Motion (Force and Acceleration)

- Principle: The acceleration of an object depends on the mass of the object and the amount of force applied (F = ma).

- Application: A lighter stone requires less force to accelerate and is easier to throw with the necessary speed and spin for multiple skips.

C. Newton's Third Law of Motion (Action and Reaction)

- Principle: For every action, there is an equal and opposite reaction.

- Application: When the stone hits the water, the water exerts an equal and opposite force back on the stone, causing it to bounce or skip.

D. Kinetic Energy

- Principle: The energy an object possesses due to its motion (KE = 0.5 * m * v²).

- Application: The faster the stone moves, the more kinetic energy it has, which helps it to overcome the water's resistance and skip multiple times.

E. Conservation of Momentum

- Principle: The total momentum of a system remains constant if no external forces act on it.

- Application: The momentum of the stone is transferred to the water surface upon impact, contributing to the stone's ability to skip.

2.1.2 Forces Involved in Stone Skipping

Several forces come into play during the act of stone skipping. Understanding these forces helps in optimizing your throw for the best results:

A. Gravity

- Description: Gravity pulls the stone downward towards the water.

- Effect: The angle of your throw must counteract gravity to keep the stone from sinking immediately. A flatter throw helps maintain the stone's trajectory above the water.

B. Lift

- Description: Lift is the force that acts perpendicular to the direction of motion of the stone, created by the pressure difference on the stone's surface as it moves.

- Effect: The lift force helps the stone to rise and skip. The shape and angle of the stone when it hits the water determine the amount of lift generated.

C. Drag

- Description: Drag is the resistance force exerted by the air and water against the stone's motion.

- Effect: Drag slows the stone down, reducing the number of skips. Minimizing drag by choosing flat, smooth stones and throwing them with a spinning motion helps increase the skips.

D. Centripetal Force

- Description: This force acts on a spinning object, keeping it stable by pulling it towards its center of rotation.

- Effect: A rapidly spinning stone maintains a stable, flat orientation, crucial for maximizing the number of skips. The spin ensures the stone doesn't tumble and lose its optimal angle upon impact with the water.

E. Buoyant Force

- Description: The upward force exerted by the water, opposing the weight of the stone.

- Effect: Buoyancy helps the stone float momentarily before it skips again. The stone's density and the water's surface tension play significant roles in this interaction.

By understanding these principles and forces, you can better control and refine your stone skipping technique. The next section will delve into the ideal angles and speeds for skipping, building on this foundational knowledge to help you achieve the perfect throw.

2.2 The Ideal Angle and Speed

Achieving the perfect stone skip requires not only the right stone and technique but also an understanding of the ideal angles and speed. This section provides a detailed guide to optimizing these critical factors for maximum skips.

2.2.1 Optimal Angles for Skipping

The angle at which you throw the stone significantly influences its ability to skip across the water. Here are the key considerations for finding the optimal angles:

A. Angle of Attack

- Principle: The angle of attack is the angle between the stone's trajectory and the surface of the water.

- Optimal Angle: Research and practical experience show that the ideal angle of attack for skipping stones is around 20 degrees. This angle balances lift and drag, allowing the stone to skip efficiently.

- Application: To achieve this angle, practice throwing the stone with a flick of your wrist, keeping it as flat and parallel to the water as possible. Visualize the stone entering the water at a shallow angle rather than a steep one.

B. Stone Orientation

- Principle: The orientation of the stone when it hits the water affects the number of skips.

- Flat Entry: The stone should strike the water with its flat side, maximizing surface contact and minimizing penetration into the water.

- Application: Hold the stone between your thumb and fingers, ensuring it is flat and level. Your release should keep the stone's flat surface parallel to the water, aiding in achieving the optimal angle of attack.

C. Adjusting for Conditions

- Wind and Waves: External conditions like wind and waves can affect the stone's trajectory and angle of attack.

- Adjustments: In windy conditions, aim slightly lower to counteract the wind lifting the stone. On wavy water, try to time your throw to coincide with the troughs of the waves for a smoother surface.

2.2.2 *Speed and Spin Dynamics*

Speed and spin are crucial elements that work together to enhance the stone's skipping potential. Understanding and mastering these dynamics will significantly improve your skipping performance.

A. Throwing Speed

- Principle: The speed at which you throw the stone directly impacts its kinetic energy and skipping capability.

- Optimal Speed: Higher speeds provide more kinetic energy, allowing the stone to skip multiple times before losing momentum.

- Application: Focus on a quick, snapping motion of your wrist to generate speed. The stone should leave your hand rapidly, with a sharp release. Practice increasing your throwing speed while maintaining control and accuracy.

B. Spin Dynamics

- Principle: Spin stabilizes the stone in flight, maintaining its flat orientation and increasing the number of skips.

- Optimal Spin: A high rate of spin is essential for stability and balance. The stone should spin rapidly, similar to a Frisbee.

- Application: To achieve optimal spin, grip the stone firmly between your thumb and fingers. As you throw, flick your wrist sharply to impart a fast spin. Your fingers should roll off the stone in a smooth, quick motion, creating a spin that stabilizes the stone in flight.

C. Balancing Speed and Spin

- Principle: The best skips are achieved by balancing both speed and spin. Too much speed without enough spin can cause the stone to tumble, while too much spin without enough speed can result in short skips.

- Application: Practice combining speed and spin in your throws. Start with slower throws to perfect your spin technique, then gradually increase speed while maintaining the same spin rate. Experiment with different combinations to find the balance that works best for you.

D. Consistency in Technique

- Practice: Consistency is key to mastering speed and spin dynamics. Regular practice helps develop muscle memory and precision.

- Routine: Create a practice routine that focuses on both speed and spin. Use markers or targets to gauge your progress and refine your technique.

By mastering the optimal angles for skipping and balancing the speed and spin of your throws, you can significantly improve your stone skipping skills. The following chapters will build on this foundation, providing further tips and advanced strategies to help you become a stone skipping expert.

2.3 Hydrodynamics

Hydrodynamics, the study of fluids in motion, is essential for understanding how a stone interacts with water and achieves multiple skips. This section provides an in-depth look at the interaction between stone and water and the impact of water surface tension on stone skipping.

2.3.1 Interaction Between Stone and Water

Understanding how a stone interacts with water is crucial for mastering the art of skipping. The following points break down the key interactions:

A. Impact Forces

- Principle: When the stone hits the water, it experiences an impact force that propels it back into the air. This force is influenced by the stone's speed, angle, and surface area.

- Optimal Impact: For optimal skipping, the stone should hit the water at a shallow angle (around 20 degrees) with sufficient speed and a flat orientation.

- Application: To achieve the ideal impact, practice throwing the stone so it makes contact with the water smoothly, without plunging deeply. A flat, rapid spin helps distribute the impact force evenly across the stone's surface, facilitating a clean skip.

B. Water Displacement

- Principle: As the stone hits the water, it displaces a small volume of water, creating a cavity or splash.

- Effect: The surrounding water rushes back to fill the cavity, pushing the stone upward and enabling it to skip.

- Application: Choose stones with a broad, flat surface to maximize water displacement and the resultant upward force. Ensure your throw imparts a balanced combination of speed and spin to maintain this interaction consistently across skips.

C. Energy Transfer

- Principle: Energy is transferred from the stone to the water upon impact, with some energy being converted to kinetic energy, helping the stone to bounce off the water's surface.

- Conservation: Efficient energy transfer ensures that more energy is retained for subsequent skips.

- Application: Practice throwing the stone with a quick, snapping motion to maximize initial kinetic energy. Monitor the stone's skips to gauge the effectiveness of your energy transfer, adjusting speed and angle as needed.

D. Hydrodynamic Lift

- Principle: Hydrodynamic lift is generated by the stone as it moves across the water's surface, similar to how an airplane wing generates lift in the air.

- Effect: This lift helps the stone to maintain its trajectory and skip multiple times.

- Application: Ensure that the stone's shape and orientation are optimized for creating lift. A flat stone thrown at the correct angle with rapid spin will generate the necessary lift to sustain multiple skips.

2.3.2 *Impact of Water Surface Tension*

Water surface tension plays a significant role in the stone skipping process. Here's how it affects your throws:

A. *Surface Tension Dynamics*

- Principle: Water surface tension acts like a thin elastic sheet on the water's surface, providing resistance against the stone's impact.

- Effect: This resistance is crucial for the stone to bounce off the surface rather than sink.

- Application: Throw the stone with sufficient speed and at the optimal angle to maximize the benefit of surface tension. A flat, spinning stone will interact more effectively with the surface tension, leading to better skips.

B. *Environmental Factors*

- Calm Water: Ideal conditions for stone skipping include calm, flat water surfaces where surface tension is uniformly distributed.

- Disturbances: Wind, waves, and ripples can disrupt surface tension, making it harder for the stone to skip.

- Application: Choose your skipping locations carefully. Look for calm, undisturbed water bodies for practice. When conditions are less than ideal, adjust your technique to compensate for disruptions, such as throwing at a slightly lower angle to counteract choppy water.

C. Temperature and Surface Tension

- Principle: Water temperature affects surface tension, with cooler water having higher surface tension than warmer water.

- Effect: Higher surface tension in cooler water can enhance skipping performance.

- Application: While you can't control water temperature, being aware of its impact can help you understand variations in your skipping results. If skipping in cooler conditions, you may find it easier to achieve multiple skips due to increased surface tension.

D. Consistency and Practice

- Routine: Consistency in your technique will help you better understand the nuances of hydrodynamics and surface tension.

- Practice: Regular practice in different conditions will help you adapt and refine your throws to achieve optimal skips regardless of environmental factors.

By mastering the interaction between stone and water and understanding the impact of surface tension, you can significantly improve your stone skipping skills. The next chapters will build on this knowledge, offering advanced tips and strategies to help you become a stone skipping expert.

Chapter 2 Review

In Chapter 2: Understanding the Science of Stone Skipping, the focus is on the scientific principles that govern stone skipping, including physics, angles, speed, and hydrodynamics. Here's a detailed review of each section:

- 2.1 The Physics of Stone Skipping

- Basic Principles of Physics: This section introduces the fundamental physics concepts relevant to stone skipping, such as motion, energy, and momentum. It lays the groundwork for understanding how these principles apply to the act of skipping stones.

- Forces Involved in Stone Skipping: Learn about the various forces at play when skipping a stone, including gravity, lift, and drag. This part explains how these forces interact to influence the stone's trajectory and number of skips.

- 2.2 The Ideal Angle and Speed

- Optimal Angles for Skipping: Discover the best angles for launching a stone to maximize the number of skips. This section provides detailed explanations and diagrams to illustrate why certain angles work better than others.

- Speed and Spin Dynamics: Understand the importance of speed and spin in achieving successful skips. Learn how to generate the right amount of speed and spin to keep the stone on the surface of the water and prolong its skipping motion.

- 2.3 Hydrodynamics

- Interaction Between Stone and Water: This section delves into the hydrodynamic principles that affect stone skipping. It explains how the stone's shape and motion interact with the water's surface to create lift and enable skipping.

- Impact of Water Surface Tension: Learn about the role of water surface tension in stone skipping. This part covers how surface tension influences the stone's ability to skip and how environmental factors like temperature and water type can affect it.

Summary

Chapter 2 provides a thorough understanding of the science behind stone skipping, covering key concepts in physics, the optimal angle and speed for skips, and the hydrodynamics involved. By grasping the basic principles of physics and the forces at play, you can better appreciate the mechanics of stone skipping. Understanding the ideal angles and speed dynamics helps improve your technique, while knowledge of hydrodynamics and water surface tension offers insights into achieving more consistent and successful skips. This chapter equips you with the scientific knowledge necessary to refine your stone skipping skills.

Chapter 3: Selecting the Perfect Stone

Choosing the right stone is essential for successful stone skipping. The type, shape, and condition of the stone significantly impact its skipping potential. This section guides you through understanding the different types of stones and identifying the best ones for skipping.

3.1 Types of Stones

Selecting the ideal stone for skipping involves understanding the characteristics of different types of stones. This section provides a detailed comparison between flat and rounded stones and highlights the best stones for skipping.

3.1.1 Flat Stones vs. Rounded Stones

A. Flat Stones

- Characteristics: Flat stones have a broad, even surface that makes contact with the water smoothly.

- Advantages:

  - Less Drag: The flat surface reduces drag, allowing the stone to glide over the water.

  - More Lift: The shape generates more lift, making the stone skip multiple times.

  - Stability: Flat stones are more stable in flight due to their even distribution of mass.

- Application: Ideal for beginners and experienced skippers, flat stones provide consistent and predictable skipping performance.

B. Rounded Stones

- Characteristics: Rounded stones have a curved, uneven surface.

- Disadvantages:

  - Higher Drag: The curved surface creates more drag, slowing the stone down quickly.

  - Less Lift: Rounded stones generate less lift, often leading to fewer skips.

  - Instability: They tend to roll and tumble, causing unpredictable skips and frequently sinking after the first impact.

- Application: Rounded stones are generally less effective for skipping and are best avoided unless no other options are available.

3.1.2 Best Stones for Skipping

A. Ideal Characteristics

1. Flatness

   - Importance: Flat stones skip better because they have a larger surface area in contact with the water, which helps in generating lift and reducing drag.

   - Visual Cue: Look for stones with an even, flat surface without significant bumps or grooves.

2. Size

- Optimal Size: Stones about the size of your palm are perfect. They are easy to grip and throw, providing a balance between control and distance.

- Guideline: Aim for stones that are roughly 2-4 inches in diameter.

3. Weight

- Balance: Medium-weight stones offer the best balance of speed and control. Too light, and they lack momentum; too heavy, and they are hard to throw effectively.

- Test: Hold the stone in your hand; it should feel substantial but not cumbersome.

4. Shape

- Preferred Shape: Oval or disc-shaped stones are optimal. These shapes ensure a smooth, consistent interaction with the water.

- Avoid: Irregular or oddly shaped stones, as they can cause erratic skips.

B. Specific Types of Stones

1. Slate

- Description: Slate stones are typically flat and smooth, making them excellent for skipping.

- Benefits: They are naturally shaped in a way that suits skipping, with minimal need for additional shaping or preparation.

2. Shale

   - Description: Shale stones are flat and come in various sizes suitable for skipping.

   - Benefits: They are lightweight and easy to handle, offering great skipping potential with minimal effort.

3. Sedimentary Rocks

   - Description: Many sedimentary rocks, like sandstone, have the ideal flatness and weight for stone skipping.

   - Benefits: These stones are abundant and often naturally smoothed by water, making them readily available for skippers.

By understanding the differences between flat and rounded stones and knowing what characteristics to look for, you can select the best stones for skipping. The following sections will guide you on where to find these stones in nature and how to prepare them for optimal performance.

3.2 Finding Stones in Nature

To find the perfect skipping stones, you need to know where to look and how to identify the best candidates. This section provides practical tips and techniques for locating and selecting ideal stones.

3.2.1 Ideal Locations for Stone Hunting

Finding good skipping stones starts with knowing the best places to look. Here are some ideal locations:

A. Riverbanks

- Description: Riverbanks are rich in smooth, flat stones due to the natural erosion process.

- Why It's Ideal: The constant flow of water over rocks smooths and shapes them into ideal skipping stones.

- Application: Look for areas where the river current is gentle, as these spots often have a higher concentration of flat stones. Focus on bends in the river where water flow slows down, depositing smooth stones.

B. Lakeshores

- Description: Shores of lakes often have an abundance of flat stones, especially in calm, shallow areas.

- Why It's Ideal: Lake shores receive stones from surrounding high grounds, which are naturally polished by wave action.

- Application: Search along the waterline where the waves have washed up stones. Pay special attention to pebbled beaches and areas with visible erosion.

C. Beaches

- Description: Coastal beaches with pebbles and rocks can be excellent places to find skipping stones.

- Why It's Ideal: Ocean waves continuously tumble stones, smoothing their surfaces and edges.

- Application: Explore areas with small, rounded pebbles, and look for flatter stones among them. Early morning or after a storm are good times to find freshly uncovered stones.

D. Creeks and Streams

- Description: Smaller bodies of water like creeks and streams also deposit flat stones along their banks.

- Why It's Ideal: The gentle flow of water in creeks and streams can create ideal skipping stones.

- Application: Focus on shallow areas and spots where the water flow slows, such as behind bends or near obstacles like fallen trees.

3.2.2 Tips for Spotting Good Skipping Stones

Once you are at an ideal location, use these tips to find the best skipping stones:

A. Visual Inspection

- Criteria: Look for stones that are flat, smooth, and free of cracks or sharp edges.

- Technique: Scan the ground methodically, paying attention to stones that stand out due to their flatness and uniform shape.

- Application: Pick up stones and turn them in your hand to check for even surfaces and appropriate thickness. Discard any that have jagged edges or are too thick.

B. Weight Test

- Method: Hold the stone in your hand to assess its weight. It should feel light enough to throw comfortably but heavy enough to have momentum.

- Guideline: Aim for stones that are neither too heavy nor too light. Medium-weight stones are generally the best for skipping.

- Application: Practice tossing a few stones to get a sense of the ideal weight. Stones that feel right in your hand and have a nice balance are usually the best.

C. Shape Selection

- Preferred Shapes: Choose stones that are disc-shaped or oval. These shapes are more aerodynamic and stable during flight.

- Avoid: Steer clear of stones with irregular shapes or uneven surfaces, as they are less likely to skip effectively.

- Application: Flat stones with a slight curve are ideal. Stones that are too round or too pointed will not skip well.

D. Surface Smoothness

- Criteria: The smoother the surface of the stone, the better it will skip.

- Technique: Run your fingers over the stone's surface to check for smoothness. Small ridges or indentations can disrupt the stone's flight.

- Application: Choose stones that feel smooth to the touch and have minimal texture. Stones with a polished or naturally smooth surface will perform best.

E. Consistency

- Principle: Consistency in your selection process will help you build a collection of reliable skipping stones.

- Technique: Develop a routine for evaluating stones based on the criteria above.

- Application: Keep a mental or written checklist of the ideal characteristics, and use it every time you go stone hunting. This will help you become more efficient and effective in finding perfect skipping stones.

By knowing where to look and how to identify the best stones, you can significantly improve your stone skipping skills. The next section will cover how to prepare your stones for skipping, ensuring they are in optimal condition for use.

3.3 Preparing Your Stones

Once you have selected your stones, proper preparation is essential to maximize their performance. This involves cleaning, shaping, and storing your stones correctly. Follow these detailed steps to prepare your stones for the best skipping experience.

3.3.1 Cleaning and Shaping

A. Cleaning

1. Purpose: Cleaning your stones removes dirt, debris, and algae that can affect their skipping performance.

2. Materials Needed: Water, a soft brush, mild soap (optional), and a clean cloth.

3. Steps:

   - Step 1: Rinse the stones under running water to remove loose dirt and debris.

   - Step 2: Use a soft brush to gently scrub the surface of each stone. Pay attention to crevices and uneven areas where dirt may be trapped.

   - Step 3: If the stones are particularly dirty, add a small amount of mild soap to the water and continue scrubbing. Rinse thoroughly to remove any soap residue.

   - Step 4: Dry the stones with a clean cloth or allow them to air dry completely before use.

B. Shaping

1. Purpose: Sometimes, natural stones may need slight adjustments to improve their skipping potential. Shaping ensures the stones have an even surface and are free of sharp edges.

2. Materials Needed: Fine-grit sandpaper or a sanding block.

3. Steps:

   - Step 1: Inspect each stone for any sharp edges or rough spots that might affect its skipping performance.

   - Step 2: Use fine-grit sandpaper to gently smooth out any rough edges or uneven surfaces. Focus on creating a uniform, flat surface.

   - Step 3: Sand in a circular motion to maintain the natural shape of the stone. Avoid over-sanding, which can alter the stone's weight and balance.

   - Step 4: After shaping, rinse the stones again to remove any dust from sanding. Dry them thoroughly before use.

3.3.2 Storing Your Stones

Proper storage is essential to maintain the condition and performance of your stones. Follow these guidelines to store your stones correctly.

A. Storage Conditions

1. Environment: Store your stones in a dry, cool place to prevent any moisture damage. Moisture can lead to mold and mildew, which can affect the stone's surface.

2. Containers: Use breathable containers like mesh bags or wooden boxes to allow air circulation. Avoid plastic bags or airtight containers, which can trap moisture.

B. Organization

1. Labeling: If you have different types of stones, consider labeling or organizing them by size and type. This makes it easier to select the right stone for different conditions and practice sessions.

2. Accessibility: Keep your stones in an easily accessible location so you can quickly grab them for practice or competitions. An organized storage system helps save time and ensures you always have the best stones ready for use.

C. Routine Maintenance

1. Inspection: Regularly inspect your stored stones for any signs of damage or wear. Remove any stones that have developed cracks or rough edges.

2. Cleaning: Periodically clean your stored stones to keep them in top condition. A quick rinse and dry can help maintain their performance over time.

By following these steps to clean, shape, and store your stones, you can ensure they remain in optimal condition for skipping. Properly prepared stones will perform better, allowing you to achieve more consistent and impressive skips. The next chapters will build on this foundation, providing advanced tips and strategies to help you become a stone skipping expert.

Chapter 3 Review: Selecting the Perfect Stone

In Chapter 3: Selecting the Perfect Stone, the focus is on identifying, finding, and preparing the best stones for skipping. Here's a detailed review of each section:

- 3.1 Types of Stones

   - Flat Stones vs. Rounded Stones: This section explains the differences between flat and rounded stones, detailing why flat stones are generally preferred for skipping. It covers how the shape affects the stone's ability to skip across the water.

   - Best Stones for Skipping: Learn about the ideal characteristics of skipping stones, such as their size, weight, and smoothness. This part provides specific examples and visuals to help you identify the best stones for successful skips.

- 3.2 Finding Stones in Nature

   - Ideal Locations for Stone Hunting: Discover the best places to find suitable skipping stones. This section highlights common locations like riverbanks, lakeshores, and beaches, and explains why these areas are rich in quality stones.

- Tips for Spotting Good Skipping Stones: Get practical advice on how to spot good skipping stones in natural settings. Tips include looking for smooth, flat stones and using tools like sieves or nets to aid in your search.

- 3.3 Preparing Your Stones

- Cleaning and Shaping: Learn how to properly clean and, if necessary, shape your stones to optimize their skipping potential. This includes removing dirt and debris, and smoothing rough edges to ensure better performance.

- Storing Your Stones: This section provides guidance on how to store your stones to keep them in good condition. Tips include using containers or bags and keeping them in a dry, safe place to avoid damage.

Summary

Chapter 3 is crucial for understanding how to select, find, and prepare the best stones for skipping. By learning the differences between flat and rounded stones, and identifying the ideal characteristics of skipping stones, you can improve your chances of successful skips. The chapter also offers practical advice on finding stones in nature, cleaning and shaping them, and storing them properly to maintain their quality. This comprehensive guide ensures you have the perfect stones ready for your next stone skipping session.

Chapter 4: Techniques for Skipping Stones

- 4.1 Basic Stone Skipping Technique

- 4.2 Advanced Skipping Techniques

- 4.3 Common Mistakes and How to Avoid Them

Mastering the art of stone skipping requires a blend of skill, technique, and practice. This chapter delves into the essential techniques needed to skip stones effectively, starting from the basics and progressing to advanced methods. By understanding and applying these techniques, you can increase your skip count, impress onlookers, and enjoy the timeless pastime of stone skipping. We will also explore common mistakes and how to avoid them to ensure your stone skipping sessions are both fun and successful.

4.1 Basic Stone Skipping Technique

Mastering the basic stone skipping technique is essential for anyone looking to improve their skip count and enjoy the sport to its fullest. This section will guide you through the fundamental steps, starting with the proper grip and stance and moving on to the wind-up and release.

4.1.1 Proper Grip and Stance

A. Proper Grip

1. *Select the Right Stone:*

   - Size and Shape: Choose a stone that is flat, smooth, and fits comfortably in your hand. The ideal stone should be about the diameter of a quarter to a half dollar, ensuring it's neither too heavy nor too light.

- Surface Texture: Look for stones with a smooth surface. Rough or uneven stones can disrupt the spin and trajectory.

2. Hold the Stone Correctly:

- Thumb Placement: Place your thumb on top of the stone, pressing it down gently to secure the stone in place.

- Index Finger Position: Curl your index finger around the edge of the stone, providing stability and control.

- Middle Finger Support: Use your middle finger to support the bottom of the stone. This creates a balanced grip that allows for a smooth release.

3. Practice the Grip:

- Consistency: Ensure that your grip is consistent with each throw. Practicing your grip regularly will help you maintain control and improve your overall technique.

B. Proper Stance

1. Position Your Feet:

- Sideways Stance: Stand sideways to the water, with your non-dominant foot closest to the water's edge. This stance helps you generate more power and control.

- Shoulder-Width Apart: Keep your feet shoulder-width apart to maintain balance and stability.

2. Balance and Posture:

- Knee Bend: Maintain a slight bend in your knees. This allows for better movement and flexibility during the throw.

- Forward Lean: Lean slightly forward from your hips. This helps you engage your core muscles and generate more power in your throw.

3. Body Relaxation:

- Stay Relaxed: Keep your body relaxed but ready to move fluidly. Tension can negatively affect your throw, so practice staying loose and agile.

4.1.2 Wind-Up and Release

A. Wind-Up

1. Arm Position:

- Starting Position: Begin with your throwing arm extended back, parallel to the ground. Your wrist should be cocked back slightly, ready for the throw.

- Elbow Bend: Keep a slight bend in your elbow to help generate momentum and control during the throw.

2. Focus and Aim:

- Visualize the Target: Keep your eyes focused on the spot where you want the stone to hit the water first. Visualizing the trajectory helps improve accuracy.

- Mental Preparation: Take a moment to mentally prepare and visualize the entire motion. This can help in executing a smooth and controlled throw.

3. Body Rotation:

- Hip and Shoulder Rotation: As you wind up, rotate your hips and shoulders to build momentum. This rotational movement is crucial for generating power and spin.

B. Release

1. Swing Motion:

- Smooth Transition: Bring your arm forward in a smooth, whipping motion. Ensure your arm moves fluidly from the wind-up position to the release.

- Body Coordination: Coordinate the movement of your hips, shoulders, and arm to generate maximum power.

2. Spin and Release:

- Wrist Snap: As your arm comes forward, snap your wrist to impart spin on the stone. The spin helps stabilize the stone and increases the number of skips.

- Release Point: Release the stone when your hand is just above hip level, aiming for a low, flat trajectory. The stone should leave your hand at a slight angle to the water's surface.

3. Follow-Through:

- Complete the Motion: Follow through with your arm after releasing the stone. A full follow-through helps maintain balance and adds power to your throw.

- Maintain Balance: Ensure you stay balanced and controlled even after the stone is released. This helps in preparing for subsequent throws and improving consistency.

By following these detailed steps, you can master the basic stone skipping technique, laying a solid foundation for more advanced skills. Remember, practice is key. Each throw provides an opportunity to refine your technique and enjoy the simple pleasure of stone skipping.

4.2 Advanced Skipping Techniques

Once you've mastered the basics of stone skipping, it's time to elevate your game with advanced techniques. This section will cover how to increase the spin and speed of your throws, as well as how to master the skip count for more impressive results.

4.2.1 Increasing Spin and Speed

A. Generating More Spin

1. Fingertip Control:

   - Grip Adjustment: Hold the stone with your thumb on top, index finger curled around the edge, and middle finger supporting the bottom. Use your fingertips to exert greater control over the stone.

   - Finger Placement: Position your index and middle fingers closer to the edge of the stone to maximize the spin.

2. Wrist Action:

   - Wrist Snap: Focus on a quick, snapping motion of your wrist as you release the stone. The faster the snap, the greater the spin imparted to the stone.

   - Practice Drills: Perform wrist snap drills by practicing the motion without releasing the stone. This helps build muscle memory and control.

3. Spin Practice:

   - Dry Runs: Practice the release motion without actually throwing the stone. Focus on the wrist snap and how it affects the stone's spin.

- Consistency: Aim for a consistent, strong spin with each practice throw. Over time, this will become a natural part of your throwing technique.

B. Boosting Speed

1. Powerful Throw:

   - Body Mechanics: Use your entire body to generate power. Start with your feet and transfer the energy through your legs, hips, torso, and arm.

   - Hip Rotation: Rotate your hips swiftly and powerfully as you bring your arm forward. This rotation is crucial for generating maximum speed.

2. Follow-Through:

   - Complete the Motion: Ensure your arm follows through completely after the release. A full follow-through helps maintain the stone's speed and trajectory.

   - Balance and Control: Stay balanced and controlled throughout the motion. A stable follow-through leads to more consistent and powerful throws.

3. Speed Drills:

   - Weighted Practice: Practice throwing with a slightly heavier stone. This builds strength and improves your ability to generate speed with a standard skipping stone.

   - Resistance Training: Incorporate resistance bands or light weights into your training routine to build arm and shoulder strength.

4.2.2 Mastering the Skip Count

A. Understanding Angles

1. Optimal Angle:

   - Release Angle: Aim to release the stone at an angle of about 20 degrees relative to the water's surface. This angle maximizes the potential for multiple skips.

   - Adjustment for Conditions: Adjust your angle based on the water conditions. For choppy water, a slightly higher angle may be necessary to achieve consistent skips.

2. Angle Practice:

   - Target Practice: Set up targets at different distances on the water's surface to practice hitting them at the correct angle. This helps develop your ability to control the release angle.

   - Visual Aids: Use visual aids like a protractor or a marked stick to help you consistently find the right release angle during practice.

B. Practicing Consistency

1. Repetition:

   - Frequent Practice: Regularly practice your throwing technique to develop muscle memory. The more you practice, the more natural the motion will become.

   - Routine: Establish a consistent practice routine, focusing on both technique and accuracy.

2. Analyzing Performance:

   - Video Analysis: Record your throws and review the footage to identify areas for improvement. Look for inconsistencies in your grip, stance, wind-up, and release.

   - Feedback: Seek feedback from experienced stone skippers or coaches. They can provide valuable insights and tips to help you refine your technique.

3. Adjustment and Improvement:

   - Iterative Process: Continuously adjust and improve your technique based on your performance analysis. Small tweaks can lead to significant improvements in your skip count.

   - Patience and Persistence: Mastering the skip count requires patience and persistence. Keep practicing and refining your skills to achieve consistent and impressive results.

By incorporating these advanced techniques into your practice, you can significantly improve your stone skipping performance. Increasing spin and speed, along with mastering the skip count, will elevate your skills and make your stone skipping sessions more enjoyable and rewarding. Remember, the key to success is consistent practice and a willingness to refine your technique continuously.

4.3 Common Mistakes and How to Avoid Them

Mastering the art of stone skipping involves not only learning the right techniques but also recognizing and correcting common mistakes. This section will guide you through identifying typical errors and provide practical tips to ensure consistent, successful skipping.

4.3.1 Identifying Errors

A. *Incorrect Grip*

1. Too Tight a Grip:

   - Problem: Holding the stone too tightly restricts wrist movement and reduces spin.

   - Solution: Maintain a firm but relaxed grip. Your thumb should press gently on top, while your fingers provide stable support.

2. Too Loose a Grip:

   - Problem: A loose grip can cause the stone to slip or wobble, affecting control and accuracy.

   - Solution: Ensure your fingers are wrapped securely around the stone without squeezing too hard.

3. Improper Finger Placement:

   - Problem: Incorrect positioning of fingers can disrupt the balance and spin of the stone.

   - Solution: Place your thumb on top, index finger curled around the edge, and middle finger supporting the bottom.

B. *Poor Stance*

1. Rigid Stance:

   - Problem: A stiff, rigid stance can limit your range of motion and reduce the power of your throw.

   - Solution: Keep your stance relaxed and flexible. Stand sideways to the water with feet shoulder-width apart.

2. Unbalanced Position:

- Problem: An unbalanced stance can lead to instability and inconsistent throws.

- Solution: Distribute your weight evenly and maintain a slight bend in your knees for better control.

C. Improper Release

1. Releasing Too High:

- Problem: Releasing the stone too high results in a steep angle, reducing the number of skips.

- Solution: Release the stone at hip level, aiming for a low, flat trajectory.

2. Releasing Too Low:

- Problem: Releasing too low can cause the stone to hit the water without skipping.

- Solution: Ensure the stone leaves your hand at the correct height and angle.

3. Lack of Spin:

- Problem: Insufficient spin causes the stone to wobble and sink quickly.

- Solution: Focus on snapping your wrist during the release to impart a strong spin.

4.3.2 Tips for Consistent Skipping

A. Grip Adjustments

1. Consistency in Grip:

- Practice Holding: Regularly practice holding the stone with a consistent grip to develop muscle memory.

- Experiment: Try slight variations in finger placement to find the most comfortable and effective grip.

2. Grip Pressure:

- Firm but Relaxed: Ensure your grip is firm enough to control the stone but relaxed enough to allow for a smooth release.

B. Stance Refinement

1. Balanced Stance:

- Stable Foundation: Maintain a stable foundation by keeping your feet shoulder-width apart and your weight evenly distributed.

- Flexibility: Stay flexible and avoid locking your knees. This helps in generating power and maintaining control.

2. Body Alignment:

- Sideways Position: Stand sideways to the water to maximize the range of motion.

- Slight Forward Lean: Lean slightly forward to engage your core muscles and generate more power.

C. Release Practice

1. Timing of Release:

- Correct Height: Practice releasing the stone at the right height (just above hip level) to achieve a low trajectory.

- Angle Control: Aim to release the stone at a 20-degree angle relative to the water's surface.

2. Spin Generation:

- Wrist Snap: Focus on snapping your wrist during the release to impart a strong spin.

- Practice Drills: Perform wrist snap drills to build muscle memory and improve spin control.

D. Regular Practice

1. Frequent Practice Sessions:

- Routine: Establish a regular practice routine to develop and maintain your skills.

- Varied Conditions: Practice in different water conditions to adapt your technique accordingly.

2. Feedback and Analysis:

- Video Analysis: Record your throws and review the footage to identify areas for improvement.

- Seek Feedback: Get feedback from experienced stone skippers to gain valuable insights and tips.

E. Patience and Persistence

1. Iterative Improvement:

   - Small Adjustments: Continuously make small adjustments based on your practice results and feedback.

   - Persistent Practice: Be patient and persistent. Consistent practice leads to gradual and sustained improvement.

By identifying common mistakes and following these practical tips, you can enhance your stone skipping skills and achieve more consistent results. Remember, the key to success lies in regular practice, attention to detail, and a willingness to refine your technique continuously. Enjoy the process and the satisfaction that comes with mastering the art of stone skipping.

Chapter 4 Review: Techniques for Skipping Stones

In Chapter 4: Techniques for Skipping Stones, the focus is on mastering both basic and advanced techniques, as well as avoiding common mistakes. Here's a detailed review of each section:

- 4.1 Basic Stone Skipping Technique

   - Proper Grip and Stance: This section provides detailed instructions on how to hold the stone correctly and position your body for optimal stability and control. It covers finger placement, body alignment, and balance to ensure a solid foundation for your skips.

   - Wind-Up and Release: Learn the essential movements for a successful skip, including how to wind up and release the stone. This part emphasizes the importance of a smooth, controlled motion and the correct release angle to achieve multiple skips.

- 4.2 Advanced Skipping Techniques

- Increasing Spin and Speed: Discover techniques to add more spin and speed to your throws, which are crucial for achieving longer distances and higher skip counts. Tips include adjusting your grip, refining your wrist flick, and enhancing your arm motion.

- Mastering the Skip Count: This section focuses on strategies to maximize the number of skips. It provides advanced tips on timing, angle adjustments, and utilizing the stone's natural properties to improve your skip count.

- 4.3 Common Mistakes and How to Avoid Them

- Identifying Errors: Learn how to recognize common mistakes that can hinder your stone skipping performance. This part helps you identify issues such as improper grip, poor stance, and incorrect release techniques.

- Tips for Consistent Skipping: Get practical advice on how to correct these errors and maintain consistency in your skips. This includes refining your technique, practicing regularly, and staying mindful of common pitfalls.

Summary

Chapter 4 is essential for mastering the art of stone skipping, covering both basic and advanced techniques. By focusing on proper grip, stance, wind-up, and release, you'll build a solid foundation. Advanced tips on increasing spin, speed, and skip count will take your skills to the next level. Additionally, learning to identify and avoid common mistakes will help you achieve consistent and successful skips. This chapter provides a comprehensive guide to perfecting your stone skipping technique.

Chapter 5: Practicing and Perfecting Your Skills

- 5.1 Setting Up Practice Sessions

- 5.2 Drills and Exercises

- 5.3 Tracking Your Progress

Perfecting your stone skipping skills requires dedication, practice, and a systematic approach. This chapter will guide you through setting up effective practice sessions, performing targeted drills and exercises, and tracking your progress to continually improve your technique.

5.1 Setting Up Practice Sessions

Effective practice sessions are crucial for mastering stone skipping. By choosing the right location and understanding the best conditions for practice, you can maximize your learning and improve your skills systematically. This section provides a detailed guide on setting up practice sessions.

5.1.1 Finding the Right Practice Spot

A. Location Selection

1. *Calm Water:*

   - Ideal Water Bodies: Look for lakes, ponds, or calm sections of rivers. Calm water is essential for accurate skipping and tracking your stone's path.

   - Avoid Rough Water: Steer clear of oceans or fast-flowing rivers where waves and currents can disrupt the stone's trajectory.

2. Open Space:

- Safety First: Ensure there is ample open space around your practice spot to avoid hitting obstacles or people.

- Clear Shoreline: Choose a location with a clear, unobstructed shoreline to provide a safe and easy throwing area.

3. Accessibility:

- Easy Access: Select a spot that is easy to reach, allowing for frequent practice sessions without much hassle.

- Convenience: Consider the proximity to your home or regular travel routes to make practice more convenient.

B. Water Access

1. Shallow Shoreline:

- Ease of Retrieval: A shallow, gently sloping shoreline makes it easier to retrieve stones and allows for better visibility of the skips.

- Clear View: Ensure the shoreline offers a clear view of the water's surface to accurately observe the stone's performance.

2. Stable Ground:

- Solid Footing: Practice on stable, solid ground to maintain good balance and posture while throwing.

- Comfort: Choose a spot with comfortable ground conditions to stand on for extended periods.

C. Environmental Considerations

1. Clean Area:

   - Debris-Free: Select a clean area free from litter and debris, which can interfere with your practice and pose safety risks.

   - Natural Beauty: Practicing in a pleasant environment can make your sessions more enjoyable and motivating.

2. Quiet Surroundings:

   - Minimize Distractions: Choose a quiet location to help you focus on your technique without interruptions.

   - Tranquility: A peaceful setting can enhance your concentration and the overall practice experience.

5.1.2 Optimal Conditions for Practice

A. Weather Conditions

1. Calm Weather:

   - Minimal Wind: Practice on days with minimal wind to ensure the stone's flight path is not disturbed.

   - Stable Weather: Avoid practicing in extreme weather conditions like heavy rain or strong winds, which can hinder your performance.

2. Clear Skies:

   - Visibility: Clear skies provide better visibility, allowing you to track the stone's skips more accurately.

   - Comfort: Practicing in good weather conditions can make your sessions more comfortable and enjoyable.

B. Time of Day

1. Morning or Evening:

- Calm Waters: Early morning or late evening often offers calmer waters and fewer disturbances.

- Quiet Times: These times are usually quieter, reducing the chances of distractions and interruptions.

2. Consistent Timing:

- Routine Development: Practicing at the same time each day helps establish a routine and allows you to track progress under consistent conditions.

- Habit Formation: Consistent practice times help in building a habit, making it easier to stick to your practice schedule.

C. Stone Selection

1. Variety of Stones:

- Different Sizes and Shapes: Bring a variety of stones to practice with, including different sizes and shapes, to adapt your technique accordingly.

- Experimentation: Experimenting with various stones can help you understand how different factors influence the skipping performance.

2. Optimal Stones:

- Ideal Characteristics: Choose stones that are flat, smooth, and fit comfortably in your hand for the best skipping results.

- Preparation: Spend some time before practice sessions selecting and preparing your stones to ensure a productive practice.

Summary

Setting up effective practice sessions is a foundational step in mastering stone skipping. By selecting the right practice spot and ensuring optimal conditions, you can create an environment conducive to learning and improvement. Calm water, an open and accessible location, and the right weather and timing all contribute to productive practice sessions. Incorporate a variety of stones to challenge and refine your technique, and establish a consistent routine to track your progress and achieve your stone skipping goals.

5.2 Drills and Exercises

To excel in stone skipping, you need to refine your technique and build the necessary strength and precision. This section provides structured drills and exercises designed to enhance your skills systematically.

5.2.1 Improving Technique and Form

A. *Grip Drills*

1. *Grip Adjustment Drill:*

   - Objective: Find the most comfortable and effective grip.

   - Steps:

     1. Select a variety of stones.

2. Hold each stone with different grips (e.g., varying finger placement and pressure).

3. Practice the release motion without throwing the stone, focusing on maintaining a consistent grip.

4. Note which grip feels most comfortable and secure.

2. Consistency Drill:

   - Objective: Maintain a consistent grip during each throw.

   - Steps:

   1. Choose your preferred grip.

   2. Hold the stone and mimic the throwing motion repeatedly without releasing the stone.

   3. Ensure that the grip remains steady throughout the motion.

   4. Gradually increase speed while maintaining consistency.

B. Stance Drills

1. Balance and Posture Drill:

   - Objective: Achieve a balanced and stable stance.

   - Steps:

   1. Stand sideways to an imaginary waterline with feet shoulder-width apart.

   2. Slightly bend your knees and lean forward from the hips.

3. Hold this position for several seconds to build muscle memory.

4. Practice moving into and out of this stance fluidly.

2. *Movement Drill:*

- Objective: Simulate the throwing motion to improve coordination.

- Steps:

1. Stand in the proper stance.

2. Perform the entire throwing motion without releasing a stone.

3. Focus on the fluid movement of your hips, shoulders, and arm.

4. Repeat several times to build muscle memory.

C. Release Drills

1. Wrist Snap Drill:

- Objective: Enhance wrist snap for better spin.

- Steps:

1. Hold the stone in your preferred grip.

2. Snap your wrist quickly while holding the stone, without releasing it.

3. Focus on the quick, snapping motion of your wrist.

4. Repeat until the motion feels natural and strong.

2. *Low Trajectory Drill:*

   - Objective: Achieve the optimal release angle.

   - Steps:

     1. Stand in the proper stance.

     2. Perform the throwing motion, releasing the stone at hip level.

     3. Aim for a low, flat trajectory, keeping the stone close to the water's surface.

     4. Practice until the motion becomes smooth and consistent.

5.2.2 Building Strength and Precision

A. Strength Training

1. Arm and Shoulder Exercises:

   - Push-Ups:

     - Objective: Build upper body strength.

     - Steps: Perform regular or modified push-ups in sets of 10-15 reps.

   - Resistance Band Workouts:

     - Objective: Strengthen arm and shoulder muscles.

     - Steps: Use resistance bands to perform exercises like bicep curls and shoulder presses, aiming for 10-15 reps per set.

2. *Core Workouts:*

- Planks:

    - Objective: Strengthen core muscles for stability.

    - Steps: Hold a plank position for 30-60 seconds, focusing on maintaining a straight line from head to heels.

- Sit-Ups:

    - Objective: Improve core strength.

    - Steps: Perform sit-ups or crunches in sets of 15-20 reps.

B. Precision Drills

1. Target Practice:

- Objective: Improve accuracy and control.

- Steps:

    1. Set up targets (e.g., floating objects or markers) at varying distances on the water.

    2. Aim to hit the targets consistently with your throws.

    3. Adjust your technique based on feedback from each throw.

    4. Gradually increase the distance and difficulty of the targets.

2. Distance Throws:

- Objective: Build strength and learn to control throw force.

- Steps:

1. Select a range of stones.

2. Practice throwing each stone at different distances, focusing on both power and precision.

3. Adjust the force of your throw to achieve the desired distance without compromising form.

4. Track your progress and aim to increase the distance over time.

C. Repetition and Consistency

1. Routine Practice:

- Objective: Develop and maintain a consistent practice routine.

- Steps:

1. Schedule regular practice sessions (e.g., daily or several times a week).

2. Focus on both technique and strength exercises during each session.

3. Ensure consistency in your practice routine to build muscle memory.

2. Varied Conditions:

- Objective: Adapt skills to different environments.

- Steps:

1. Practice in different weather conditions and water environments (e.g., calm lakes, windy days).

2. Adjust your technique based on the conditions.

3. Learn to adapt quickly and maintain performance regardless of the environment.

Summary

By following these structured drills and exercises, you can systematically improve your stone skipping technique, build the necessary strength, and achieve greater precision. Regular practice, combined with targeted drills, will help you refine your skills and become a proficient stone skipper. Remember, consistent effort and attention to detail are key to mastering the art of stone skipping.

5.3 Tracking Your Progress

Tracking your progress is a critical component of improving your stone skipping skills. By systematically recording your practice sessions and analyzing your performance, you can identify areas for improvement and set achievable goals. This section outlines the best practices for keeping a skipping log and effectively analyzing your performance.

5.3.1 Keeping a Skipping Log

A. Recording Sessions

1. Log Book Setup:

   - Choose a Format: Decide whether you want to use a physical notebook or a digital log. Digital logs can be more flexible and easier to analyze.

   - Create Sections: Divide your log into sections for each practice session, including date, location, weather conditions, and specific notes.

2. Detailing Each Session:

   - Date and Time: Record the date and time of each practice session to track your progress over time.

   - Location: Note the specific location of your practice to see how different environments affect your performance.

   - Weather Conditions: Include details about the weather, such as wind speed, temperature, and water conditions, as these factors can influence your skipping results.

3. Recording Performance:

   - Number of Skips: Record the number of skips achieved with each throw.

   - Types of Stones: Note the types of stones used, including size, shape, and weight.

   - Technique Used: Detail the specific technique or grip you used for each throw.

B. Progress Tracking

1. Skip Count Tracking:

   - Average Skips: Calculate the average number of skips per session to monitor improvements.

   - Best Performance: Record your best skip count for each session to set benchmarks and goals.

2. Technique Notes:

   - Adjustments Made: Note any adjustments to your technique, stance, or grip, and how these changes affected your performance.

   - Observations: Include any observations about what worked well and what didn't during the session.

3. Reviewing Logs:

   - Regular Review: Regularly review your skipping log to identify trends and patterns in your performance.

   - Set Goals: Use the information in your log to set specific, achievable goals for future practice sessions.

5.3.2 Analyzing Your Performance

A. Video Analysis

1. Recording Throws:

   - Setup: Use a smartphone or camera to record your throws from different angles.

   - Multiple Angles: Record from the side and front to get a comprehensive view of your technique.

2. Reviewing Footage:

   - Slow Motion: Watch the recordings in slow motion to carefully analyze your grip, stance, and release.

   - Identify Issues: Look for any inconsistencies or errors in your technique, such as improper grip, poor stance, or incorrect release angle.

3. Feedback and Improvement:

   - Seek Expert Advice: Share your recordings with experienced stone skippers or coaches for constructive feedback.

   - Implement Changes: Use the feedback to make precise adjustments to your technique and practice routine.

B. Benchmarking

1. Set Performance Benchmarks:

   - Initial Assessment: Use your initial practice sessions to set baseline benchmarks for skip count, technique consistency, and accuracy.

   - Progressive Goals: Establish progressive goals based on your benchmarks, such as increasing your average skip count by a certain percentage or improving accuracy with specific types of stones.

2. Track Improvements:

   - Regular Updates: Regularly update your benchmarks as you improve. Compare your current performance with past records to see how much progress you've made.

   - Adjust Goals: Adjust your goals based on your progress. If you achieve a goal sooner than expected, set a new, more challenging goal.

3. *Continuous Improvement:*

   - Iterative Process: Continuously refine your technique and practice routine based on your performance analysis.

   - Stay Motivated: Use your progress as motivation to keep practicing and improving. Celebrate milestones and achievements along the way.

Summary

Keeping a detailed skipping log and analyzing your performance are essential practices for any serious stone skipper. By systematically recording your practice sessions and reviewing your progress, you can identify areas for improvement and set realistic, achievable goals. Regular video analysis and feedback from experienced skippers can further refine your technique and help you achieve greater consistency and success. Remember, the key to mastery is continuous practice, reflection, and adjustment.

Chapter 5 Review: Practicing and Perfecting Your Skills

In Chapter 5: Practicing and Perfecting Your Skills, the focus is on honing your stone skipping abilities through effective practice and monitoring your progress. Here's a detailed review of each section:

- 5.1 Setting Up Practice Sessions

   - Finding the Right Practice Spot: This section guides you on selecting the best location for your practice sessions. It emphasizes finding calm water surfaces, such as lakes or ponds, and ensuring the area is free from obstacles like rocks or debris that could interfere with your skips. Accessibility and convenience for regular practice are also considered.

- Optimal Conditions for Practice: Learn about the ideal environmental conditions for stone skipping, including calm weather, minimal wind, and smooth water surfaces. Practicing during daylight hours for better visibility is recommended. These conditions help in achieving more consistent and successful skips.

- 5.2 Drills and Exercises

- Improving Technique and Form: Discover specific drills designed to refine your technique and improve your form. Detailed instructions are provided on how to position your fingers on the stone, maintain the proper stance for stability, and achieve the optimal release angle. These drills are aimed at enhancing your skipping performance.

- Building Strength and Precision: Engage in exercises that focus on building the necessary strength and precision for successful stone skipping. This includes workouts to strengthen your throwing arm, such as resistance training and flexibility exercises, and activities to improve hand-eye coordination, like target practice with different stone sizes and weights.

- 5.3 Tracking Your Progress

- Keeping a Skipping Log: Understand the importance of maintaining a log to track your practice sessions. This involves noting down key details such as the date and time of practice, the number of skips achieved, the distance covered, and any observations about your performance. A structured template for recording this information is suggested to help you stay organized and consistent.

- Analyzing Your Performance: Learn how to review and analyze your skipping log to identify areas of improvement. This section provides tips on how to interpret your data, look for patterns or trends in your performance, set specific goals for future sessions, and measure your progress over time. Techniques for visualizing your data, such as creating charts or graphs, are also discussed to make the analysis more intuitive and insightful.

Summary

Chapter 5 emphasizes the importance of structured practice and consistent tracking to perfect your stone skipping skills. By setting up ideal practice conditions, engaging in targeted drills, and meticulously tracking your progress, you can continually refine your technique and achieve better results. This chapter provides practical advice and detailed instructions to help you make the most out of your practice sessions and monitor your development effectively.

Chapter 6: Competing in Stone Skipping

- 6.1 Local and National Competitions

- 6.2 Rules and Regulations

- 6.3 Strategies for Winning

Competing in stone skipping can be a thrilling and rewarding experience. Whether you're participating in local events or aiming for national competitions, understanding how to find and prepare for competitions, knowing the rules, and employing effective strategies can greatly enhance your performance. This chapter will guide you through everything you need to know about competing in stone skipping.

6.1 Local and National Competitions

Competing in stone skipping can add a new level of excitement and challenge to your practice. This section will guide you through finding local and national competitions and preparing effectively for your first competition.

6.1.1 Finding Competitions Near You

A. Research and Resources

1. Local Clubs and Organizations:

   - Stone Skipping Clubs: Join local stone skipping clubs or organizations, which often host competitions and have information about upcoming events.

- Community Centers: Check with local community centers, as they may organize or have information about stone skipping competitions.

2. *Online Platforms:*

- Websites and Forums: Use stone skipping websites, forums, and social media groups to find competition listings and updates. Sites dedicated to stone skipping often have event calendars and forums where enthusiasts share information.

- Social Media: Follow stone skipping pages and groups on social media platforms like Facebook, Instagram, and Twitter for the latest news on competitions.

3. *Parks and Recreation Departments:*

- Local Events: Contact parks and recreation departments to inquire about annual stone skipping events or local competitions held at public parks and lakes.

4. *Networking:*

- Meet Fellow Enthusiasts: Attend local stone skipping meetups and practice sessions to network with other enthusiasts who can inform you about competitions.

- Word of Mouth: Engage with the stone skipping community to learn about competitions through word of mouth.

B. Community Centers and Parks

1. *Local Events:*

- Annual Competitions: Many community centers and parks host annual stone skipping competitions. These events are often publicized through local bulletins, websites, and social media.

- Family-Friendly Events: Look for family-friendly events that encourage participation from all age groups, providing a fun and supportive environment for competitors.

2. Bulletin Boards:

   - Flyers and Announcements: Check bulletin boards at local libraries, sporting goods stores, and community centers for flyers and announcements about upcoming stone skipping competitions.

6.1.2 Preparing for Your First Competition

A. *Understand the Format*

1. Event Structure:

   - Number of Rounds: Learn about the number of rounds and how they are structured. Some competitions may have preliminary rounds followed by finals.

   - Scoring System: Understand the scoring system, including how skips are counted and any bonus points or penalties.

2. Categories:

   - Age Groups and Skill Levels: Determine the categories you are eligible to compete in, such as age groups (e.g., junior, adult) or skill levels (e.g., amateur, professional).

3. Registration:

   - Entry Requirements: Familiarize yourself with the entry requirements, including registration deadlines, fees, and necessary paperwork. Register early to secure your spot in the competition.

B. Practice and Training

1. Regular Practice:

- Consistent Routine: Establish a consistent practice routine, dedicating time to refine your technique and build endurance.

- Simulation: Practice under conditions similar to those expected at the competition, such as the type of water body and weather conditions.

2. Specific Drills:

- Technique Drills: Focus on drills that enhance your grip, stance, and release. Consistent practice will help solidify these fundamental skills.

- Strength and Precision: Incorporate strength training and precision drills to improve your throwing power and accuracy.

C. Gather Equipment

1. Stone Selection:

- Variety of Stones: Bring a variety of stones that you have practiced with and feel comfortable using. Different conditions may require different types of stones.

- Preferred Stones: Select stones that are flat, smooth, and fit comfortably in your hand for the best skipping performance.

2. Gear:

- Appropriate Clothing: Wear comfortable clothing suitable for the weather conditions. Consider layers if the weather is unpredictable.

- Accessories: Bring sunscreen, hats, and sunglasses for sun protection. Pack water and snacks to stay hydrated and energized.

D. Mental and Physical Preparation

1. Stay Healthy:

- Proper Diet: Maintain a healthy diet to ensure you have the energy and stamina needed for the competition.

- Exercise: Regular exercise will help you stay in good physical condition, improving your overall performance.

2. Mental Focus:

- Visualization: Practice visualization techniques, imagining successful throws and perfect skips to build confidence.

- Relaxation Techniques: Use relaxation techniques such as deep breathing exercises to stay calm and composed during the competition.

Summary

Preparing for stone skipping competitions involves thorough research, regular practice, and mental and physical preparation. By finding local and national competitions, understanding the format, practicing diligently, gathering the right equipment, and preparing mentally and physically, you can enhance your chances of success. Enjoy the excitement and challenge of competing, and remember that every competition is an opportunity to learn and improve.

6.2 Rules and Regulations

Competing in stone skipping requires a thorough understanding of the rules and a commitment to fair play and sportsmanship. This section will guide you through the essential competition rules and the importance of maintaining good sportsmanship.

6.2.1 *Understanding Competition Rules*

A. General Rules

1. Entry Requirements:

   - Registration: Ensure you register for the competition by the stated deadline. Check for any registration fees and necessary paperwork.

   - Eligibility: Verify your eligibility for specific categories based on age, skill level, or other criteria.

2. Stone Specifications:

   - Size and Weight: Competitions may specify the size and weight of the stones used. Typically, stones should be flat and smooth, fitting comfortably in your hand.

   - Material: Ensure the stones are made from permissible materials. Some compctitions may have restrictions on the type of stones allowed.

3. Number of Stones:

   - Allowed Stones: Know the number of stones you are allowed to use in each round. Competitions usually specify the number of stones you can skip within a given timeframe.

B. Competition Conduct

1. Throwing Techniques:

   - Permissible Techniques: Understand the allowed throwing techniques. Most competitions allow a side-arm throw, but check for any specific restrictions.

   - Prohibited Actions: Be aware of any prohibited actions, such as overhand throws or the use of artificial aids.

2. Scoring System:

   - Skip Count: Learn how skips are counted. Typically, a skip is counted each time the stone touches the water surface before sinking.

   - Distance: Some competitions may score based on the distance the stone travels, in addition to the number of skips.

   - Bonus Points: Check if there are any bonus points for exceptional performances, such as the longest distance or highest number of skips.

3. Penalties:

   - Infractions: Familiarize yourself with common infractions and their corresponding penalties. This could include using disallowed stones or violating throwing techniques.

   - Disqualifications: Understand the actions that could lead to disqualification, such as unsportsmanlike conduct or repeated rule violations.

C. Event-Specific Rules

1. Unique Regulations:

   - Specific Competitions: Each competition may have unique rules. Always read the event-specific regulations provided by the organizers.

   - Time Limits: Some competitions may have time limits for each throw or round. Ensure you are aware of these constraints.

2. Judge's Decisions:

   - Authority: Respect the decisions made by judges and officials. Their rulings are typically final and based on the competition's established rules.

6.2.2 Fair Play and Sportsmanship

A. Respect Competitors

1. Conduct:

   - Respectful Bchavior: Always maintain a respectful and courteous attitude towards fellow competitors, organizers, and spectators.

   - Encouragement: Encourage and support other participants, fostering a positive and friendly competitive environment.

2. Etiquette:

   - Wait Your Turn: Respect the turn order and wait patiently for your chance to throw.

   - Applaud Success: Applaud the successes of others, acknowledging their efforts and achievements.

B. Adherence to Rules

1. Follow Regulations:

   - Rule Compliance: Strictly adhere to all competition rules and regulations to ensure fair play.

   - Honesty: Be honest in your performance, accurately reporting your results and any mistakes.

2. Integrity:

   - True to the Sport: Compete with integrity, upholding the values of stone skipping and setting a good example for others.

C. Handling Disputes

1. Resolve Peacefully:

   - Calm Dispute Resolution: Handle any disputes or disagreements in a calm and respectful manner.

   - Official Channels: Use official channels and procedures to address any issues or appeals.

2. Accept Outcomes:

   - Gracious Acceptance: Accept the outcomes of the competition graciously, whether you win or lose.

   - Learning Opportunity: View each competition as a learning opportunity, regardless of the result.

Summary

Understanding the rules and regulations of stone skipping competitions is essential for fair and successful participation. By familiarizing yourself with the general rules, specific competition conduct, and event-specific regulations, you can compete effectively and with confidence. Additionally, upholding the principles of fair play and sportsmanship ensures a positive and enjoyable experience for all participants. Respect your competitors, adhere to the rules, and handle disputes gracefully to contribute to the integrity and spirit of stone skipping competitions.

6.3 Strategies for Winning

Winning a stone skipping competition requires more than just technical skills. It involves mental preparation and the application of competitive techniques that enhance your performance under pressure. This section provides a step-by-step guide to mastering the mental and technical aspects of competition.

6.3.1 Mental Preparation

A. Visualization Techniques

1. Mental Imagery:

   - Create a Mental Picture: Regularly practice visualization by creating a detailed mental image of a successful throw. Imagine the stone leaving your hand, skipping perfectly across the water, and achieving multiple skips.

   - Sensory Involvement: Engage all your senses in the visualization. Feel the weight of the stone, hear the sound of it hitting the water, and see the ripples created by each skip.

2. Scenario Planning:

   - Anticipate Challenges: Visualize different competition scenarios, including potential challenges such as wind or uneven water surfaces. Plan your responses to these situations.

   - Positive Outcomes: Focus on positive outcomes, reinforcing confidence and reducing anxiety.

B. Focus and Concentration

1. Mindfulness Practices:

   - Meditation: Practice mindfulness meditation to enhance your focus and concentration. Spend a few minutes each day sitting quietly, focusing on your breath, and clearing your mind of distractions.

   - Body Awareness: Develop body awareness by paying attention to how your body feels during practice. This helps you maintain proper form and technique.

2. Eliminate Distractions:

   - Mental Focus: Train your mind to block out distractions during practice and competition. Techniques such as deep breathing and mental counting can help maintain focus.

   - Controlled Environment: Create a controlled practice environment that minimizes distractions, allowing you to concentrate fully on your technique.

C. Stress Management

1. Relaxation Techniques:

   - Deep Breathing: Practice deep breathing exercises to calm your mind and body. Inhale deeply through your nose, hold for a few seconds, and exhale slowly through your mouth.

   - Progressive Muscle Relaxation: Use progressive muscle relaxation to reduce tension. Gradually tense and then relax each muscle group, starting from your toes and working up to your head.

2. Positive Thinking:

   - Affirmations: Use positive affirmations to boost your confidence. Repeat phrases such as "I am a skilled stone skipper" or "I perform well under pressure."

   - Focus on Strengths: Concentrate on your strengths and past successes to build confidence and reduce anxiety.

6.3.2 Competitive Techniques

A. Optimizing Throwing Technique

1. Refine Technique:

   - Consistent Practice: Continuously practice your throwing technique, focusing on maintaining a consistent grip, stance, and release. Regular practice helps develop muscle memory.

   - Feedback: Seek feedback from experienced skippers or coaches to identify areas for improvement. Make necessary adjustments to refine your technique.

2. Adapt to Conditions:

- Environmental Adaptation: Learn to adapt your throwing technique to different environmental conditions, such as wind, water currents, and surface types. Practice under various conditions to become more versatile.

- Flexible Strategy: Develop a flexible strategy that allows you to adjust your technique quickly based on the competition environment.

B. Strategic Stone Selection

1. Stone Variety:

- Bring Options: Bring a variety of stones to the competition, including different sizes, shapes, and weights. This allows you to choose the best stone for the specific conditions.

- Test Conditions: Test different stones during practice sessions leading up to the competition to determine which ones perform best under expected conditions.

2. Practice with Preferred Stones:

- Familiarity: Regularly practice with your preferred stones to build familiarity and confidence. Knowing how a particular stone behaves increases your control and precision.

- Backup Stones: Always have backup stones ready in case your primary stone gets lost or damaged.

C. Consistency and Precision

1. Focus on Consistency:

- Steady Performance: Aim for consistent performance rather than occasional spectacular throws. Consistent skips are more likely to result in higher scores.

- Routine Practice: Develop a routine practice schedule that emphasizes consistency in every aspect of your technique.

2. Precision Drills:

- Target Practice: Set up targets at various distances on the water and practice hitting them accurately. This improves your precision and control.

- Controlled Throws: Practice controlled throws where you focus on hitting a specific point on the water. Gradually increase the difficulty of your targets to enhance precision.

Summary

Winning a stone skipping competition involves both mental and technical preparation. By using visualization techniques, improving focus and concentration, managing stress, refining your throwing technique, strategically selecting stones, and emphasizing consistency and precision, you can enhance your performance and increase your chances of success. Consistent practice and a positive mindset are key to mastering the art of stone skipping and excelling in competitions.

Chapter 6 Review: Competing in Stone Skipping

Competing in stone skipping can enhance your skills and provide a thrilling experience. Chapter 6 covers finding competitions, understanding the rules, and strategies for winning. Here's a summary of the key points.

6.1 Local and National Competitions

Finding Competitions Near You:

- Research: Look for local and national stone skipping competitions through online searches, community bulletin boards, and local community centers.

- Networking: Connect with local stone skipping clubs and groups to learn about upcoming competitions.

Preparing for Your First Competition:

- Understand the Format: Familiarize yourself with the event structure, scoring system, and specific rules.

- Practice and Training: Establish a consistent practice routine and focus on technique, strength, and precision.

- Gather Equipment: Bring a variety of stones and wear appropriate clothing. Pack necessary gear like sunscreen, water, and snacks.

- Mental and Physical Preparation: Maintain a healthy lifestyle, practice mental techniques, and stay focused and calm.

6.2 Rules and Regulations

Understanding Competition Rules:

- General Rules: Ensure registration is complete, verify stone specifications, and know the permissible throwing techniques.

- Competition Conduct: Understand how skips are counted and the scoring system used. Be aware of penalties and actions that could lead to disqualification.

- Event-Specific Rules: Familiarize yourself with unique rules for each competition, respect judges' decisions, and follow all guidelines.

Fair Play and Sportsmanship:

- Respect Competitors: Maintain a respectful attitude toward fellow competitors and spectators.

- Adherence to Rules: Follow all competition rules and regulations to ensure fair play.

- Handling Disputes: Resolve disputes calmly and respectfully, using official channels for any appeals. Accept outcomes graciously and learn from each event.

6.3 Strategies for Winning

Mental Preparation:

- Visualization Techniques: Practice visualizing successful throws and positive outcomes.

- Focus and Concentration: Engage in mindfulness practices and develop techniques to block out distractions.

- Stress Management: Use relaxation techniques and positive affirmations to build confidence and stay calm.

Competitive Techniques:

- Optimizing Throwing Technique: Continuously refine your throwing technique and adapt to different environmental conditions.

- Strategic Stone Selection: Bring a variety of stones and practice with your preferred ones to build familiarity and confidence.

- Consistency and Precision: Aim for consistent performance, focusing on reliable skips over occasional spectacular throws. Incorporate precision drills into your practice.

Summary

Competing in stone skipping requires thorough preparation, a deep understanding of the rules, and effective strategies for success. By finding competitions, preparing diligently, adhering to rules, and employing mental and competitive techniques, you can enhance your performance and enjoy the thrill of competition. Remember, the key to success lies in consistent practice, respectful sportsmanship, and continuous improvement.

Chapter 7: The Community of Stone Skipping

- 7.1 Connecting with Fellow Enthusiasts

- 7.2 Events and Gatherings

- 7.3 Promoting the Sport

Stone skipping is more than just a solitary hobby; it's a vibrant community where enthusiasts can share their passion, learn from each other, and promote the sport. This chapter explores how to connect with fellow stone skippers, participate in events, and advocate for the sport.

7.1 Connecting with Fellow Enthusiasts

Connecting with other stone skipping enthusiasts can greatly enhance your experience and improve your skills. This section covers how to join clubs and groups and engage with online communities and forums dedicated to stone skipping.

7.1.1 Joining Clubs and Groups

A. Finding Local Clubs

1. *Research:*

   - Online Searches: Use search engines to find local stone skipping clubs. Keywords like "stone skipping club near me" or "local stone skipping groups" can yield good results.

   - Community Bulletin Boards: Check bulletin boards at community centers, libraries, and local sporting goods stores for information about local stone skipping clubs.

2. *Community Centers:*

- Local Listings: Inquire at community centers and parks and recreation departments. They often have information on local clubs and groups.

- Event Calendars: Review event calendars posted at these centers to find upcoming stone skipping events and meetings.

B. Membership Benefits

1. *Skill Improvement:*

- Learning from Experts: Clubs often have experienced skippers who can offer valuable tips and feedback.

- Organized Practice: Regular practice sessions organized by the club can help you maintain a steady practice routine and continuously improve your skills.

2. *Regular Practice:*

- Scheduled Sessions: Clubs typically schedule regular practice sessions, ensuring you have consistent opportunities to practice.

- Varied Locations: Practicing at different locations with the club can help you adapt to various water conditions.

3. *Networking:*

- Meet Enthusiasts: Connect with other enthusiasts who share your passion for stone skipping.

- Community Building: Being part of a club fosters a sense of community and belonging.

C. Participation

1. Attend Meetings:

   - Stay Informed: Regularly attend club meetings to stay updated on upcoming events, competitions, and practice sessions.

   - Active Engagement: Engage actively in discussions and activities to make the most of your membership.

2. Volunteer:

   - Event Organization: Volunteer to help organize events and activities. This is a great way to contribute to the community and build stronger connections.

   - Mentorship: Offer to mentor new members, sharing your knowledge and helping them improve their skills.

7.1.2 Online Communities and Forums

A. Finding Online Communities

1. Social Media:

   - Facebook Groups: Join stone skipping groups on Facebook to connect with a large community of enthusiasts. Search for groups like "Stone Skipping Enthusiasts" or "Rock Skipping Club."

   - Instagram: Follow hashtags like #StoneSkipping and #RockSkipping to find and connect with other skippers. Participate in discussions and share your posts.

2. Specialized Forums:

   - Dedicated Websites: Participate in forums dedicated to stone skipping, such as those found on specialized stone skipping websites.

- Reddit: Join subreddit communities like r/StoneSkipping to engage in discussions, share tips, and post your achievements.

B. Engaging with the Community

1. Ask Questions:

- Seek Advice: Use online platforms to ask questions about techniques, stone selection, or finding local events.

- Participate in Discussions: Engage in discussions to learn from others' experiences and share your own insights.

2. Share Content:

- Videos and Photos: Post videos and photos of your stone skipping sessions to showcase your skills and receive feedback.

- Stories: Share stories about your stone skipping experiences, such as memorable skips or challenges you've overcome.

C. Learning and Sharing

1. Tutorials and Tips:

- Access Resources: Use online tutorials, instructional videos, and written guides shared by the community to improve your skills.

- Share Knowledge: Contribute your own tips and tutorials to help others in the community.

2. Global Network:

- Connect Internationally: Engage with stone skippers from around the world, learning about different techniques and traditions.

- Cultural Exchange: Exchange ideas and experiences, broadening your understanding and appreciation of the sport.

Summary

Connecting with fellow stone skipping enthusiasts through local clubs and online communities offers numerous benefits. Joining clubs and groups provides opportunities for skill improvement, regular practice, and networking, while online communities and forums offer a global platform for learning, sharing, and engaging with the broader stone skipping community. By actively participating in these communities, you can enhance your stone skipping experience, continuously improve your skills, and enjoy the camaraderie of fellow enthusiasts.

7.2 Events and Gatherings

Attending and hosting events can significantly enhance your stone skipping experience by providing opportunities to compete, learn, and socialize with fellow enthusiasts. This section covers how to attend stone skipping festivals and how to host your own skipping event.

7.2.1 Attending Stone Skipping Festivals

A. Finding Festivals

1. Event Listings:

- Online Searches: Use search engines to find stone skipping festivals. Search terms like "stone skipping festival" or "rock skipping events" can help you find upcoming festivals.

- Official Websites: Visit the websites of stone skipping organizations, which often list events and festivals. These sites may include detailed information about dates, locations, and registration.

2. *Local Events:*

- Community Boards: Check community bulletin boards at local libraries, community centers, and parks for announcements of local stone skipping events.

- Recreation Departments: Contact local parks and recreation departments, which may organize or have information on local stone skipping festivals and competitions.

B. Participating in Festivals

1. *Competitions:*

- Register Early: Ensure you register for competitions well in advance. Check for any entry fees and specific entry requirements.

- Compete: Take part in competitions to test your skills against others and experience the excitement of competitive stone skipping.

2. *Workshops:*

- Learn New Techniques: Attend workshops and demonstrations led by experienced skippers. These sessions provide valuable insights into advanced techniques and tips for improvement.

- Hands-On Practice: Participate in hands-on practice sessions where you can try new skills under the guidance of experts.

3. *Socializing:*

- Meet Fellow Enthusiasts: Use the festival as an opportunity to meet and interact with fellow stone skipping enthusiasts. Share stories, tips, and experiences.

- Networking: Build a network of friends and contacts who share your passion for stone skipping. This can lead to future meetups and collaborative events.

C. Travel and Accommodation

1. Plan Ahead:

   - Travel Arrangements: Book your travel arrangements well in advance to secure the best rates and ensure availability. Consider carpooling with fellow skippers to save costs and enjoy the journey together.

   - Accommodation: Look for accommodation options close to the festival location. Book early to ensure you have a convenient place to stay.

2. Explore:

   - Local Attractions: Take the opportunity to explore the local area while attending the festival. Visit nearby attractions and enjoy the culture and scenery.

   - Extend Your Stay: Consider extending your stay to relax and enjoy more stone skipping practice in different settings.

7.2.2 Hosting Your Own Skipping Event

A. Planning the Event

1. Set a Date and Location:

   - Choose a Date: Select a date that provides ample time for planning and promotion. Avoid scheduling conflicts with other local events to maximize attendance.

- Find a Suitable Location: Choose a location with calm water and ample space for participants. Public parks with lakes or ponds are ideal.

2. *Permissions:*

- Obtain Permits: Check with local authorities to see if you need any permits or permissions to host your event. This may include permission to use public spaces or organize a large gathering.

- Compliance: Ensure your event complies with all local regulations and guidelines, including safety measures and environmental considerations.

B. *Organizing Activities*

1. *Competitions and Challenges:*

- Create Categories: Organize competitions with different categories such as age groups, skill levels, and unique challenges (e.g., longest skip, most skips).

- Prizes: Offer prizes for winners to encourage participation and add excitement to the event.

2. *Demonstrations:*

- Invite Experts: Arrange demonstrations by skilled skippers to showcase advanced techniques and inspire participants.

- Interactive Sessions: Include interactive sessions where attendees can ask questions and receive hands-on tips from experts.

3. *Workshops:*

- Beginner Workshops: Offer workshops for beginners to teach the basics of stone skipping, including grip, stance, and release techniques.

- Advanced Workshops: Provide advanced workshops for experienced skippers to refine their skills and learn new techniques.

C. *Promoting the Event*

1. Marketing:

- Social Media: Use social media platforms to promote your event. Create event pages on Facebook, share updates on Instagram, and post details in relevant groups and forums.

- Flyers and Posters: Distribute flyers and posters in local community centers, libraries, sporting goods stores, and other places frequented by potential participants.

2. Invitations:

- Local Clubs and Groups: Invite local stone skipping clubs and groups to participate. Reach out to their members directly or through club newsletters.

- Word of Mouth: Encourage participants to invite their friends and family. Word of mouth can be an effective way to boost attendance.

Summary

Attending and hosting stone skipping events can significantly enhance your experience and skill development. Festivals provide opportunities to compete, learn, and socialize with other enthusiasts, while hosting your own event allows you to share your passion with the community. By carefully planning and promoting these activities, you can contribute to the growth of the stone skipping community and create memorable experiences for all participants.

7.3 Promoting the Sport

Promoting stone skipping involves not only sharing the joy of the sport with others but also advocating for its practice in environmentally responsible ways. This section explores effective methods for teaching stone skipping and advocating for its conservation and responsible practice.

7.3.1 Teaching Others

A. Formal Classes

1. Community Centers:

   - Organize Classes: Contact local community centers and propose stone skipping classes. Offer to teach both beginner and advanced levels.

   - Curriculum Development: Develop a structured curriculum that covers the basics, intermediate techniques, and advanced skills. Include practical sessions and theoretical knowledge about the sport.

2. Schools:

   - Introduce the Sport: Approach local schools to introduce stone skipping as part of their physical education or extracurricular activities.

   - Educational Programs: Create educational programs that not only teach the techniques but also include lessons on the physics of skipping stones and the environmental importance of natural water bodies.

B. Informal Teaching

1. Family and Friends:

- Teach Basics: During family outings or gatherings, teach the basics of stone skipping to friends and family. Demonstrate the proper grip, stance, and release.

- Organize Mini-Events: Host mini stone skipping events at family gatherings or picnics to engage everyone and make learning fun.

2. Public Demonstrations:

- Host Demonstrations: Organize public demonstrations at local parks or beaches. Set up a small area where passersby can watch and participate.

- Interactive Sessions: Encourage onlookers to join and try skipping stones under your guidance. Provide tips and feedback to help them improve.

C. Creating Resources

1. Tutorial Videos:

- Produce Videos: Create and share tutorial videos online that demonstrate different stone skipping techniques. Include step-by-step instructions for beginners and advanced tips for experienced skippers.

- Engage Viewers: Make your videos engaging by incorporating slow-motion clips, detailed explanations, and answering common questions.

2. Instructional Guides:

- Write Guides: Write detailed instructional guides and articles for websites, blogs, and magazines. Cover a range of topics from the basics of stone skipping to advanced techniques and competition preparation.

- Distribute Materials: Distribute these guides through local libraries, community centers, and online platforms to reach a broader audience.

7.3.2 Advocacy and Conservation

A. *Promoting Environmental Responsibility*

1. Clean Practice Areas:

- Organize Clean-Ups: Organize clean-up activities at your favorite stone skipping locations. Encourage participants to leave the area cleaner than they found it.

- Lead by Example: Always clean up after yourself and encourage others to do the same, promoting a culture of environmental responsibility within the stone skipping community.

2. Sustainable Practices:

- Use Natural Stones: Advocate for the use of natural stones instead of artificial or potentially harmful materials. Explain the environmental impact of using synthetic materials.

- Respect Wildlife: Teach skippers to respect wildlife and avoid disturbing natural habitats while practicing stone skipping.

B. Advocating for the Sport

1. Local Authorities:

- Engage with Authorities: Work with local authorities to establish designated stone skipping areas. This can help minimize conflicts with other recreational activities and protect natural sites.

- Promote the Sport: Advocate for the inclusion of stone skipping in local recreational programs and events.

2. Community Engagement:

- Organize Events: Organize community events that promote stone skipping, such as festivals, competitions, and workshops. Use these events to raise awareness about the sport and its benefits.

- Educational Outreach: Reach out to local schools, community centers, and youth organizations to introduce stone skipping as a fun and educational activity.

C. Conservation Efforts

1. Protect Waterways:

- Participate in Clean-Ups: Get involved in or organize clean-up activities to protect local waterways. Keep these areas clean to ensure they remain suitable for stone skipping.

- Support Conservation Initiatives: Support local and national conservation initiatives that aim to protect natural water bodies and their surrounding environments.

2. Environmental Education:

- Teach Conservation: Educate others about the importance of preserving natural water bodies and their ecosystems. Incorporate conservation messages into your stone skipping classes and events.

- Promote Sustainable Practices: Encourage the use of sustainable practices when it comes to choosing skipping locations and materials. Highlight the connection between enjoying the sport and taking care of the environment.

Summary

Promoting stone skipping involves teaching others the joy of the sport and advocating for its practice in an environmentally responsible manner. By organizing formal and informal teaching sessions, creating educational resources, promoting environmental responsibility, and engaging with the community, you can help grow the sport and ensure it is practiced sustainably. Embrace the role of a mentor and advocate to inspire others and protect the natural beauty that makes stone skipping possible.

Chapter 7 Review: The Community of Stone Skipping

Stone skipping is not just an individual activity; it's also a community endeavor. Chapter 7 explores how to connect with fellow enthusiasts, participate in events, and promote the sport. Here's a summary of the key points.

7.1 Connecting with Fellow Enthusiasts

Joining Clubs and Groups:

- Finding Local Clubs: Search online, check community bulletin boards, and contact local community centers to find stone skipping clubs.

- Membership Benefits: Improve your skills, participate in regular practice sessions, and connect with like-minded individuals.

- Participation: Attend meetings, volunteer for activities, and engage actively in club events to build stronger community ties.

Online Communities and Forums:

- Finding Online Communities: Join stone skipping groups on social media platforms like Facebook and Instagram, and participate in specialized forums and Reddit communities.

- Engaging with the Community: Ask questions, share experiences, and post videos and photos of your stone skipping adventures.

- Learning and Sharing: Access tutorials, tips, and discussions to improve your skills and connect with skippers worldwide.

7.2 Events and Gatherings

Attending Stone Skipping Festivals:

- Finding Festivals: Look for listings online and through stone skipping organizations, and check local event calendars.

- Participating in Festivals: Compete in events, attend workshops, and socialize with fellow enthusiasts.

- Travel and Accommodation: Plan ahead, book travel and accommodation early, and take the opportunity to explore new places.

Hosting Your Own Skipping Event:

- Planning the Event: Choose a date and location, obtain necessary permits, and ensure a safe and comfortable environment.

- Organizing Activities: Include competitions, challenges, demonstrations, and workshops for different skill levels.

- Promoting the Event: Use social media, flyers, and local media to promote the event and invite local clubs and enthusiasts.

7.3 Promoting the Sport

Teaching Others:

- Formal Classes: Offer classes at community centers and schools, and create structured curriculums for different skill levels.

- Informal Teaching: Teach family and friends during outings, and host public demonstrations to attract new enthusiasts.

- Creating Resources: Produce tutorial videos and write instructional guides to share online and through local publications.

Advocacy and Conservation:

- Promoting Environmental Responsibility: Encourage clean practice areas, use of natural stones, and respect for wildlife.

- Advocating for the Sport: Work with local authorities to establish designated stone skipping areas and engage the community through events and educational programs.

- Conservation Efforts: Participate in or organize clean-up activities, protect waterways, and educate others about environmental stewardship.

Summary

Stone skipping as a community activity offers numerous opportunities to connect with fellow enthusiasts, participate in events, and promote the sport. By joining clubs and online communities, attending or hosting events, teaching others, and advocating for environmental responsibility, you can enrich your stone skipping experience and help grow the community. Embrace the camaraderie and shared passion within the stone skipping community and enjoy the journey of continuous learning and connection.

Chapter 8: Stone Skipping for All Ages

- 8.1 Teaching Kids to Skip Stones

- 8.2 Stone Skipping as a Family Activity

- 8.3 Stone Skipping for Seniors

Stone skipping is a timeless activity that can be enjoyed by people of all ages, from young children to seniors. This chapter explores how to teach kids to skip stones, make stone skipping a fun family activity, and adjust techniques for older adults.

8.1 Teaching Kids to Skip Stones

Introducing children to the art of stone skipping can spark a lifelong love for this enjoyable and skillful activity. By simplifying techniques and ensuring safety, you can make their experience positive and memorable.

8.1.1 Simplified Techniques for Children

A. Selecting the Right Stone:

1. Size and Weight:

   - Choose Small Stones: Select smaller, lighter stones that are easy for children to hold and throw.

   - Comfortable Grip: Ensure the stone fits comfortably in the child's hand to allow better control.

2. Shape:

   - Flat and Smooth: Look for flat, smooth stones as they skip more easily across the water.

- Avoid Sharp Edges: Ensure the stones have no sharp edges to prevent injuries.

B. Basic Grip and Stance:

1. Grip:

- Thumb on Top: Teach children to place their thumb on top of the stone.

- Fingers Around Edge: Instruct them to curl their fingers around the edges of the stone for a secure hold.

2. Stance:

- Feet Shoulder-Width Apart: Have children stand with their feet shoulder-width apart for balance.

- Non-Dominant Foot Forward: Position the non-dominant foot slightly forward to provide stability during the throw.

C. Simple Throwing Technique:

1. Arm Motion:

- Side-Arm Throw: Encourage a simple side-arm throw, similar to throwing a frisbee, which is easier for children to execute.

- Practice Without Stone: Have them practice the throwing motion without a stone first to get comfortable with the movement.

2. Release Point:

- Low Angle Release: Teach children to release the stone at a low angle, just above the water's surface, to maximize skips.

- Timing: Help them practice the timing of their release to achieve the best skips.

D. Practice Makes Perfect:

1. Frequent Practice:

   - Regular Sessions: Provide plenty of opportunities for practice in a relaxed setting to build confidence.

   - Consistency: Encourage regular practice to help them develop their skills steadily.

2. Positive Reinforcement:

   - Praise Efforts: Always praise their efforts and successes, no matter how small, to build their confidence and enthusiasm.

   - Encouragement: Offer constructive feedback and encourage them to keep trying, emphasizing fun over perfection.

8.1.2 Safety Tips for Young Skippers

A. Supervision:

1. Close Supervision:

   - Constant Watch: Always supervise young children closely while they are near water to ensure their safety.

   - Stay Engaged: Actively participate in their activities to provide immediate assistance if needed.

2. *Safe Distance:*

   - Space Between Skippers: Ensure children maintain a safe distance from each other to avoid accidental injuries from flying stones.

   - Designated Areas: Set up designated areas for throwing stones to keep everyone safe and organized.

B. *Safe Environment:*

1. *Calm Waters:*

   - Choose Suitable Locations: Select practice locations with calm, shallow waters to minimize risks and make it easier for children to retrieve stones.

   - Avoid Rough Waters: Avoid fast-moving rivers or deep waters that can pose hazards.

2. *Clear Area:*

   - Free of Obstacles: Ensure the area is free of obstacles and debris that could cause tripping or injury.

   - Safe Footing: Choose areas with stable, non-slippery ground where children can stand securely.

C. *Proper Attire:*

1. *Appropriate Clothing:*

   - Comfortable and Weather-Appropriate: Dress children in comfortable, weather-appropriate clothing to keep them comfortable and focused.

- Non-Slip Footwear: Use non-slip footwear to prevent falls, especially near wet surfaces.

2. Safety Gear:

- Life Jackets: Consider life jackets for younger children, especially if they are near deeper water.

- Protective Gear: Ensure they wear hats, sunglasses, and sunscreen for protection from the sun.

D. Hydration and Sun Protection:

1. Stay Hydrated:

- Regular Water Breaks: Encourage regular water breaks to keep hydrated, especially on hot days.

- Carry Water Bottles: Bring water bottles for easy access to hydration during practice.

2. Sun Protection:

- Use Sunscreen: Apply sunscreen to protect children's skin from sunburn.

- Wear Hats and Sunglasses: Provide hats and sunglasses to protect against sun exposure and glare.

Summary

Teaching kids to skip stones can be a rewarding experience for both the instructor and the child. By simplifying techniques and ensuring safety, you can help children enjoy and succeed in this delightful activity. Select appropriate stones, teach a basic grip and stance, and focus on a simple throwing technique to get them started. Always prioritize safety through close supervision, a safe environment, proper attire, and adequate hydration and sun protection. With positive reinforcement and regular practice, children will develop their stone skipping skills and build a lasting love for this timeless pastime.

8.2 Stone Skipping as a Family Activity

Stone skipping is a wonderful way to bring the family together for fun and bonding. Engaging in games and building traditions around stone skipping creates lasting memories and strengthens family ties. This section covers fun games and challenges for family stone skipping, as well as how to build family traditions around this enjoyable activity.

8.2.1 Fun Games and Challenges

A. Skip Count Competition

1. Rules:

   - Objective: The goal is to achieve the highest number of skips in a single throw.

   - Setup: Each participant selects a stone and takes turns throwing it. A judge or another participant counts the skips.

   - Scoring: Keep track of each person's highest number of skips.

2. Variations:

   - Timed Rounds: Set a timer and see how many skips each person can achieve within a set time.

   - Team Competition: Form teams and combine the skips of each team member to determine the winning team.

3. Encouragement:

- Cheer Each Other On: Encourage family members to cheer each other on and celebrate each skip.

- Positive Feedback: Provide positive feedback and tips for improvement to help everyone enhance their skills.

B. Target Practice

1. Floating Targets:

- Setup: Place floating targets (such as small buoys or floating rings) at various distances on the water.

- Objective: The goal is to hit the targets with your stone.

2. Scoring:

- Points System: Assign points based on the difficulty and distance of the targets. Closer targets may be worth fewer points, while distant or smaller targets may be worth more.

- Keep Score: Track each participant's points to determine the winner.

3. Challenges:

- Moving Targets: Add a challenge by using targets that move with the water current.

- Timed Shots: Set a time limit for each shot to add an element of urgency and excitement.

C. Distance Throw

1. Furthest Throw:

- Objective: Compete to see who can throw the stone the farthest while maintaining good skipping technique.

- Setup: Mark the starting point and measure the distance each stone travels.

2. Scoring:

- Measuring Distance: Use a measuring tape or marked rope to determine the distance of each throw.

- Combine with Skips: Add a twist by combining the distance and the number of skips to calculate the score.

3. Practice:

- Technique: Focus on improving both distance and the number of skips through regular practice.

- Strength: Encourage strength-building exercises to enhance throwing power.

D. Creative Challenges

1. Trick Shots:

- Invent Shots: Challenge family members to invent trick shots or unique throwing styles and then attempt to replicate them.

- Examples: Examples include underhand throws, backward throws, or skipping stones through small gaps.

2. Obstacle Courses:

- Setup: Create mini obstacle courses on the water using floating objects. The objective is to navigate the stone through or around these obstacles.

- Scoring: Award points for successfully navigating the course and for style and creativity.

3. Family Fun:

- Encourage Creativity: Allow children to come up with their own challenges and games, fostering creativity and engagement.

- Rotate Challenges: Rotate who gets to choose the challenge to keep the games varied and interesting.

8.2.2 Building Family Traditions

A. Regular Outings

1. Weekly or Monthly Trips:

- Schedule: Set a regular schedule for family stone skipping outings, such as once a week or once a month.

- Favorite Spots: Visit favorite stone skipping locations and explore new ones to keep the outings exciting.

2. Combine Activities:

- Picnics: Bring along a picnic to enjoy after a stone skipping session.

- Other Games: Incorporate other outdoor games and activities to make the outing a full day of fun.

3. Rain or Shine:

   - All-Weather Gear: Prepare for various weather conditions with appropriate gear so that outings can happen rain or shine.

   - Indoor Alternatives: Have indoor activities planned in case of inclement weather, such as watching stone skipping videos or practicing throws in a safe indoor space.

B. Family Trophies

1. Skipping Trophies:

   - Create Trophies: Make homemade trophies or certificates for various achievements, such as most skips, best technique, or most improved.

   - Award Ceremonies: Hold fun award ceremonies to celebrate family members' accomplishments, adding an element of recognition and pride.

2. Rotating Trophies:

   - Challenge Winners: Use rotating trophies that the winner keeps until the next outing, encouraging friendly competition.

   - Record Names: Record the names and achievements of winners on the trophy to create a family legacy.

3. Creative Awards:

   - Unique Categories: Create unique award categories, such as "Best Skip Dance" or "Most Creative Throw," to ensure everyone has a chance to win.

C. Storytelling

1. Shared Stories:

- Memorable Moments: Share stories about past stone skipping adventures and memorable moments during family gatherings.

- Lessons Learned: Discuss lessons learned from both successes and challenges to inspire and motivate each other.

2. Family Journal:

- Document Outings: Keep a family journal of stone skipping outings, recording dates, locations, and highlights.

- Photos and Drawings: Include photos, drawings, and mementos to create a visual and written record of your family's stone skipping journey.

3. Pass Down Traditions:

- Generational Stories: Pass down stories and techniques from one generation to the next, creating a sense of continuity and tradition.

- Annual Events: Establish annual family stone skipping events or reunions to maintain the tradition over the years.

D. Teaching Tradition

1. Passing Skills:

- Teach Younger Members: Encourage older children and adults to teach younger family members the art of stone skipping.

- Mentorship: Create opportunities for older family members to mentor the younger ones, fostering a sense of responsibility and pride.

2. *Legacy Building:*

   - Family Competitions: Organize family competitions and challenges that involve all generations, emphasizing fun and learning.

   - Cultural Exchange: Share and learn about different stone skipping techniques and traditions from other cultures, enriching your family's experience.

3. *Celebrating Progress:*

   - Track Improvement: Celebrate the progress and improvement of each family member over time.

   - Continuous Learning: Encourage continuous learning and experimentation with new techniques and styles.

Summary

Stone skipping as a family activity offers numerous opportunities for fun, bonding, and building lasting traditions. By engaging in fun games and challenges, such as skip count competitions, target practice, distance throws, and creative challenges, families can enjoy quality time together while improving their skills. Building family traditions around regular outings, storytelling, and teaching younger generations ensures that the joy of stone skipping is passed down and cherished for years to come. Embrace the family spirit and make stone skipping a memorable and beloved activity for all ages.

8.3 Stone Skipping for Seniors

Stone skipping is an enjoyable and beneficial activity for seniors. It offers a gentle form of exercise, mental stimulation, and an opportunity for social interaction. This section covers how to adjust techniques for older adults and the various benefits stone skipping can provide.

8.3.1 Adjusting Techniques for Older Adults

Adapting stone skipping techniques for older adults involves making the activity comfortable, safe, and enjoyable. Here are practical steps to help seniors skip stones effectively.

A. Stone Selection

1. Lightweight Stones:

- Ease of Use: Choose lighter stones that require less effort to throw, reducing strain on the arms and shoulders.

- Variety: Provide a variety of sizes and shapes to find the most comfortable option for each individual.

2. Comfortable Grip:

- Smooth Surface: Select stones with a smooth surface to ensure a comfortable grip.

- Fit: Ensure the stones fit comfortably in the hand, allowing for a secure hold without excessive squeezing.

B. Modified Grip and Stance

1. Grip:

- Relaxed Hold: Encourage a relaxed grip to minimize strain on the hands and wrists.

- Thumb and Finger Placement: Place the thumb on top and curl the fingers around the stone, ensuring a balanced and secure hold.

2. *Stance:*

- Stable Position: Stand with feet slightly wider than shoulder-width apart to provide a stable base.

- Gentle Bend: Maintain a gentle bend in the knees to enhance balance and reduce the risk of falls.

C. Gentle Throwing Technique

1. *Arm Motion:*

- Side-Arm Throw: Use a gentle, side-arm throw to minimize strain on the shoulder and arm. The motion should be smooth and controlled.

- Practice Without Stone: Practice the throwing motion without a stone to build confidence and muscle memory.

2. *Release Point:*

- Low Angle: Focus on a low-angle release to achieve effective skips with less force.

- Smooth Release: Emphasize a smooth release to avoid jerking movements that could cause discomfort.

D. Adapted Practice

1. *Frequent Breaks:*

- Avoid Fatigue: Take regular breaks to avoid fatigue and maintain comfort. Short, frequent practice sessions are more beneficial than long, tiring ones.

- Hydration: Ensure adequate hydration during practice sessions.

2. *Supportive Environment:*

   - Comfortable Seating: Practice in locations with comfortable seating nearby, allowing for rest breaks as needed.

   - Safe Terrain: Choose practice areas with stable, non-slippery terrain to reduce the risk of falls.

8.3.2 Benefits of Stone Skipping for Seniors

Stone skipping offers numerous physical, mental, social, and emotional benefits for seniors. Engaging in this activity can enhance overall well-being and quality of life.

A. *Physical Benefits*

1. *Gentle Exercise:*

   - Low-Impact Activity: Stone skipping provides a low-impact form of exercise that is easy on the joints and suitable for seniors.

   - Improves Strength: Regularly throwing stones helps improve arm strength and coordination.

2. *Flexibility and Balance:*

   - Enhances Flexibility: The motions involved in stone skipping help maintain and improve flexibility in the arms and shoulders.

   - Promotes Balance: Adopting a stable stance and practicing controlled throws enhance balance and stability.

B. Mental Benefits

1. Stress Relief:

- Relaxing Activity: Stone skipping offers a relaxing and meditative experience, reducing stress and promoting mental well-being.

- Mindfulness: Focusing on the rhythm and technique of skipping stones fosters mindfulness and present-moment awareness.

2. Cognitive Stimulation:

- Mental Engagement: Planning and executing throws stimulate cognitive functions, keeping the mind active.

- Problem-Solving: Adjusting techniques and strategies to achieve better skips involves problem-solving and critical thinking.

C. Social Benefits

1. Community Engagement:

- Group Activities: Participating in group stone skipping activities encourages social interaction and community engagement.

- New Friendships: Meeting other enthusiasts can lead to new friendships and a sense of belonging.

2. Family Bonding:

- Quality Time: Stone skipping provides an opportunity for quality time with family members, bridging generational gaps.

- Shared Enjoyment: Enjoying a shared activity strengthens family bonds and creates lasting memories.

D. Emotional Benefits

1. Joy and Satisfaction:

- Sense of Achievement: Successfully skipping stones brings joy and a sense of accomplishment, boosting self-esteem.

- Fun and Enjoyment: The simple pleasure of stone skipping adds fun and enjoyment to everyday life.

2. Positive Outlook:

- Mental Well-Being: Engaging in a positive, enjoyable activity promotes a positive outlook and enhances mental well-being.

- Reduces Loneliness: Social interactions during stone skipping activities help reduce feelings of loneliness and isolation.

Summary

Stone skipping is a rewarding and beneficial activity for seniors, offering physical, mental, social, and emotional advantages. By adjusting techniques to suit older adults, such as selecting lightweight stones, adopting a relaxed grip and stable stance, and using gentle throwing motions, seniors can enjoy stone skipping comfortably and safely. The activity promotes gentle exercise, cognitive stimulation, social interaction, and emotional well-being, making it an excellent addition to a healthy and fulfilling lifestyle. Encourage seniors to take up stone skipping to experience its many benefits and the simple joy it brings.

Chapter 8 Review: Stone Skipping for All Ages

Stone skipping is a versatile activity that can be enjoyed by people of all ages. Chapter 8 covers how to teach kids to skip stones, make it a fun family activity, and adapt techniques for seniors. Here's a summary of the key points.

8.1 Teaching Kids to Skip Stones

Simplified Techniques for Children:

- Selecting the Right Stone: Choose small, lightweight, and flat stones that are easy for kids to hold.

- Basic Grip and Stance: Teach kids to grip the stone with their thumb on top and fingers around the edges. Stand with feet shoulder-width apart and the non-dominant foot slightly forward.

- Simple Throwing Technique: Use a side-arm throw, similar to skipping a frisbee. Release the stone at a low angle just above the water's surface.

- Practice Makes Perfect: Provide regular practice opportunities and use positive reinforcement to build confidence.

Safety Tips for Young Skippers:

- Supervision: Always closely supervise children near water and ensure they maintain a safe distance from others.

- Safe Environment: Choose calm, shallow waters and ensure the area is free of obstacles and debris.

- Proper Attire: Dress children in comfortable, weather-appropriate clothing and non-slip footwear. Consider life jackets for younger children near deeper water.

- Hydration and Sun Protection: Encourage regular water breaks and use sunscreen, hats, and sunglasses for sun protection.

8.2 Stone Skipping as a Family Activity

Fun Games and Challenges:

- Skip Count Competition: Compete to achieve the highest number of skips in a single throw. Track each person's highest skip count.

- Target Practice: Set up floating targets at various distances and assign points for hitting them.

- Distance Throw: Compete to see who can throw the stone the farthest while maintaining good technique.

- Creative Challenges: Invent trick shots and create mini obstacle courses on the water for added fun.

Building Family Traditions:

- Regular Outings: Schedule regular family stone skipping outings and combine them with picnics or other outdoor activities.

- Family Trophies: Create homemade trophies for various achievements and hold fun award ceremonies.

- Storytelling: Share memorable moments and keep a family journal of stone skipping outings.

- Teaching Tradition: Encourage older children and adults to teach younger family members, creating a sense of tradition and legacy.

8.3 Stone Skipping for Seniors

Adjusting Techniques for Older Adults:

- Stone Selection: Choose lightweight stones with a smooth surface that fit comfortably in hand.

- Modified Grip and Stance: Use a relaxed grip to minimize strain and stand with feet slightly wider than shoulder-width apart for stability.

- Gentle Throwing Technique: Use a gentle, side-arm throw to minimize strain. Focus on a smooth release at a low angle.

- Adapted Practice: Take regular breaks to avoid fatigue and practice in locations with comfortable seating and safe terrain.

Benefits of Stone Skipping for Seniors:

- Physical Benefits: Provides a low-impact form of exercise that improves arm strength, coordination, flexibility, and balance.

- Mental Benefits: Offers a relaxing and meditative experience, reducing stress and promoting mental well-being. Engages the mind in planning and executing throws.

- Social Benefits: Encourages social interaction and community engagement. Provides opportunities for quality time with family.

- Emotional Benefits: Brings joy and a sense of accomplishment. Enhances mental well-being and reduces feelings of loneliness and isolation.

Summary

Stone skipping is an inclusive activity that can be enjoyed by people of all ages. Teaching kids, engaging in family activities, and adapting techniques for seniors all contribute to making stone skipping a fun and beneficial pastime. Simplify techniques for children, ensure safety, create family traditions, and adapt practices for seniors to foster a love for stone skipping across generations. Enjoy the art of stone skipping and share its joy with your family and community.

Chapter 9: Conclusion

- 9.1 Reflecting on Your Stone Skipping Journey

- 9.2 Staying Engaged with Stone Skipping

- 9.3 The Legacy of Stone Skipping

As we reach the conclusion of the "HowExpert Guide to Stone Skipping," it's time to reflect on your journey, celebrate your progress, and look forward to the future. Stone skipping is not just a hobby; it's a lifelong pursuit that offers joy, challenge, and a deep connection to nature and community. This conclusion will help you reflect on your achievements, set new goals, stay engaged with the sport, and think about the legacy you leave for future generations.

9.1 Reflecting on Your Stone Skipping Journey

As you reach the end of your journey through the "HowExpert Guide to Stone Skipping," it's essential to take a moment to reflect on your experiences, celebrate your progress, and set goals for the future. This section will guide you through these important steps, ensuring that your passion for stone skipping continues to grow and evolve.

9.1.1 Celebrating Your Progress

Reflecting on your achievements in stone skipping is a vital part of maintaining motivation and enjoying the process. Here's how to effectively celebrate your progress:

A. Acknowledge Milestones:

1. Personal Achievements:

   - Record Your Best Throws: Keep a detailed log of your best skips, longest distances, and any personal records you've achieved. Note the dates and locations to track your progress over time.

   - Note Improvements: Reflect on how your technique, consistency, and confidence have improved since you started. Recognize the hard work and practice that contributed to these advancements.

2. Overcoming Challenges:

   - Recognize Growth: Acknowledge the challenges you've faced, such as difficult weather conditions, technical difficulties, or competition nerves. Reflect on how you've overcome these obstacles.

   - Celebrate Resilience: Celebrate your resilience and perseverance. Every step you've taken, even the difficult ones, has contributed to your growth and skill development.

B. Share Your Success:

1. Family and Friends:

   - Showcase Skills: Demonstrate your stone skipping skills to family and friends. Organize a small gathering or informal competition to share your achievements.

   - Organize Events: Host an event where you can celebrate together. Use this opportunity to engage others in the sport and share your passion.

2. *Community Engagement:*

   - Join Competitions: Participate in local or national stone skipping competitions. Competing is a great way to gain recognition for your skills and meet fellow enthusiasts.

   - Social Media: Share your achievements on social media platforms. Connect with the stone skipping community online, post videos and photos of your best skips, and celebrate milestones publicly.

9.1.2 Setting Future Goals

Setting future goals keeps your stone skipping journey dynamic and fulfilling. Here's how to establish meaningful and achievable goals:

A. Personal Development:

1. Skill Improvement:

   - Advanced Techniques: Set specific goals to learn and master advanced stone skipping techniques. Break these down into manageable steps, focusing on one aspect of your technique at a time.

   - Consistency: Aim to increase your consistency by setting targets for the number of skips per throw. Track your progress and adjust your practice routines to achieve these targets.

2. Fitness and Strength:

   - Physical Conditioning: Incorporate exercises that improve your strength, flexibility, and overall fitness. Focus on exercises that enhance your arm strength, shoulder flexibility, and core stability.

- Regular Practice: Commit to a regular practice schedule. Consistency is key to maintaining and improving your skills, so set aside dedicated time for practice each week.

B. Community Involvement:

1. Mentorship:

- Teach Others: Share your knowledge and passion by teaching stone skipping to beginners. Offer to mentor new skippers in your community, providing guidance and encouragement.

- Organize Workshops: Host workshops or informal gatherings where you can help others improve their skills. Use these events to foster a supportive and engaged stone skipping community.

2. Event Participation:

- Attend More Events: Make it a goal to attend more stone skipping events, both locally and nationally. Participate in as many competitions and gatherings as possible to gain experience and network with other enthusiasts.

- Host Events: Consider organizing your own stone skipping competitions or social events. These can be great opportunities to bring people together, promote the sport, and showcase your leadership skills.

Summary

Reflecting on your stone skipping journey involves celebrating your progress and setting future goals. Acknowledge your milestones and successes, share your achievements with family, friends, and the broader community, and set specific, achievable goals to continue improving your skills. By doing so, you'll maintain your passion for stone skipping, continuously develop your abilities, and contribute to the growth and vitality of the stone skipping community.

Embrace the journey, enjoy the process, and keep striving for new heights in the art of stone skipping.

9.2 Staying Engaged with Stone Skipping

Staying engaged with stone skipping ensures that the activity remains a source of joy, challenge, and growth. By continually learning and improving your skills, and exploring new locations, you can keep your passion for stone skipping vibrant and dynamic.

9.2.1 Continual Learning and Improvement

Engagement with stone skipping is a continuous process that involves seeking out new knowledge, refining techniques, and pushing your boundaries. Here's how to maintain a steady path of improvement:

A. Educational Resources:

1. Books and Articles:

   - Read Widely: Continue reading books and articles about stone skipping to gain new insights and techniques. Look for publications by experienced skippers or sport scientists that delve into the mechanics of skipping stones.

   - Subscribe to Magazines: Subscribe to outdoor sports and hobby magazines that feature articles on stone skipping and related activities. These resources often provide valuable tips and inspiration.

2. Online Tutorials:

- Watch Videos: Regularly watch tutorial videos on platforms like YouTube to learn new techniques and tips. Many experienced skippers share their methods and secrets through detailed video tutorials.

- Join Forums: Participate in online forums and discussion groups dedicated to stone skipping. Engage with other enthusiasts, ask questions, and share your own experiences to learn from the community.

B. Skill Enhancement:

1. Advanced Techniques:

- Experiment: Experiment with different throwing techniques and styles to enhance your skills. Try variations in grip, stance, and release angles to see what works best for you.

- Practice Drills: Incorporate practice drills that focus on specific aspects of stone skipping, such as improving spin, accuracy, or distance. Structured practice sessions help target and refine particular skills.

2. Feedback and Improvement:

- Seek Feedback: Ask for feedback from experienced skippers to identify areas for improvement. Join local clubs or participate in workshops where you can receive constructive criticism and guidance.

- Self-Assessment: Regularly assess your performance by recording and analyzing your throws. Use video recordings to spot areas needing improvement and track your progress over time.

9.2.2 Exploring New Locations

Exploring new locations keeps the stone skipping experience fresh and exciting. It challenges you to adapt to different environments and introduces you to new scenic and practice opportunities.

A. Local Exploration:

1. Discover New Spots:

   - Nearby Locations: Explore new stone skipping locations near your home. Look for different lakes, rivers, or beaches to practice at.

   - Varied Conditions: Practice in varied conditions, such as calm lakes, fast-flowing rivers, or coastal areas, to improve your adaptability and skills.

2. Community Recommendations:

   - Ask for Suggestions: Ask other enthusiasts for recommendations on good stone skipping spots. Local groups or clubs often know hidden gems that are perfect for practice.

   - Join Local Groups: Join local outdoor or stone skipping groups to discover new practice locations and meet fellow skippers.

B. Travel and Adventure:

1. Plan Trips:

   - Destination Skipping: Plan trips specifically for stone skipping, visiting renowned locations known for their perfect skipping conditions. Research places famous for their scenic beauty and ideal stone skipping waters.

- Combine Activities: Combine stone skipping with other outdoor activities like hiking, camping, or fishing. This makes the trip more diverse and enjoyable.

2. *International Locations:*

- Global Exploration: Consider traveling to international destinations famous for stone skipping. Experience different cultures and environments while practicing your skills in new settings.

- Cultural Exchange: Engage with local communities and learn about their stone skipping traditions and techniques. This cultural exchange can provide new perspectives and enrich your practice.

Summary

Staying engaged with stone skipping involves a commitment to continual learning and exploring new locations. By seeking out educational resources, refining your techniques, and pushing your boundaries, you can keep your passion for stone skipping alive and thriving. Exploring new locations, both locally and internationally, adds excitement and variety to your practice, challenging you to adapt and grow. Embrace the journey of continual improvement and adventure, and let your love for stone skipping lead you to new heights and horizons.

9.3 The Legacy of Stone Skipping

Stone skipping is more than just a skill; it's a tradition that can be passed down through generations, creating lasting memories and inspiring future enthusiasts. This section focuses on how to preserve the legacy of stone skipping by teaching it to others and motivating new generations to take up the practice.

9.3.1 Passing Down the Tradition

Passing down the tradition of stone skipping involves sharing your knowledge and enthusiasm with others, ensuring that the art continues to thrive.

A. Family Involvement:

1. Teach Younger Generations:

  - Family Bonding: Spend time teaching your children or grandchildren the art of stone skipping. Use these moments to bond and share stories about your own experiences.

  - Create Traditions: Establish regular family outings for stone skipping. Make it a tradition to visit your favorite spots and practice together.

2. Storytelling:

  - Share Stories: Share anecdotes and memorable moments from your stone skipping journey with younger family members. These stories can inspire and motivate them.

  - Document Achievements: Keep a family log of stone skipping achievements and memorable events. Include photos, drawings, and notes to create a visual and written record of your family's history with the sport.

B. Community Engagement:

1. Mentorship:

  - Guide Beginners: Offer mentorship to newcomers in the stone skipping community. Provide guidance, tips, and encouragement to help them develop their skills.

- Share Knowledge: Regularly share your knowledge and tips with others through workshops, online forums, and local gatherings.

2. *Organize Events:*

   - Host Competitions: Organize local stone skipping competitions to promote the sport and bring the community together. Create different categories for various skill levels to ensure everyone can participate.

   - Public Demonstrations: Conduct public demonstrations at parks, beaches, or community events to showcase stone skipping and inspire others to try it.

9.3.2 *Inspiring Future Generations*

Inspiring future generations to take up stone skipping involves educational outreach and promoting environmental stewardship, ensuring that the sport continues to grow and thrive.

A. *Educational Outreach:*

1. *Schools and Camps:*

   - Introduce in Schools: Work with local schools to introduce stone skipping as a fun and educational activity. Offer to teach classes or run workshops during physical education sessions.

   - Summer Camps: Collaborate with summer camps to include stone skipping in their programs. This can help children develop a love for the sport during their formative years.

2. *Youth Organizations:*

   - Scout Groups: Partner with scout groups or other youth organizations to teach stone skipping and promote outdoor activities. Offer to run sessions or provide materials for leaders to use.

- After-School Programs: Offer after-school programs focused on stone skipping and outdoor exploration. These programs can provide a structured environment for children to learn and practice.

B. Environmental Stewardship:

1. Promote Conservation:

- Teach Responsibility: Educate others about the importance of preserving natural water bodies and practicing environmental responsibility. Highlight the connection between enjoying the sport and taking care of the environment.

- Organize Clean-Ups: Lead or participate in clean-up activities at stone skipping locations to protect the environment. Encourage participants to leave areas cleaner than they found them.

2. Advocate for Sustainability:

- Support Conservation Efforts: Advocate for local and national conservation efforts that protect natural water bodies. Engage with environmental organizations to promote sustainable practices within the stone skipping community.

- Raise Awareness: Raise awareness about the environmental impact of outdoor activities and promote sustainable practices. Use your platform, whether through social media or community events, to spread the message of conservation.

Summary

The legacy of stone skipping lies in its ability to be passed down and inspire future generations. By involving your family, engaging with the community, and focusing on educational outreach and environmental stewardship, you can ensure that stone skipping continues to be a beloved activity for years to come. Embrace the role of a mentor and advocate, sharing your passion and knowledge with others to keep the tradition alive and thriving. Inspire others to take up stone skipping, and contribute to the preservation and growth of this timeless art.

Chapter 9 Review: Conclusion

As we conclude the "HowExpert Guide to Stone Skipping," it's important to reflect on your journey, stay engaged with the sport, and think about the legacy you'll leave. This chapter helps you celebrate your progress, set future goals, and inspire future generations.

9.1 Reflecting on Your Stone Skipping Journey

Celebrating Your Progress:

- Acknowledge Milestones: Keep a log of your best skips, longest distances, and personal records. Recognize the challenges you've overcome and celebrate your resilience.

- Share Your Success: Share your skills with family and friends through small gatherings or informal competitions. Participate in local or national competitions and connect with the community on social media.

Setting Future Goals:

- Personal Development: Set goals to learn advanced techniques and increase consistency. Incorporate exercises to improve strength and flexibility, and commit to regular practice.

- Community Involvement: Teach beginners, offer mentorship, and organize workshops. Attend more events and consider hosting your own competitions or social gatherings.

9.2 Staying Engaged with Stone Skipping

Continual Learning and Improvement:

- Educational Resources: Read books and articles, subscribe to magazines, watch tutorial videos, and join online forums to learn new techniques and engage with other enthusiasts.

- Skill Enhancement: Experiment with different throwing techniques and use practice drills to focus on specific skills. Seek feedback from experienced skippers and regularly assess your performance.

Exploring New Locations:

- Local Exploration: Discover new stone skipping spots near your home and practice in varied conditions. Ask for recommendations from other enthusiasts and join local groups.

- Travel and Adventure: Plan trips to renowned stone skipping locations and combine skipping with other outdoor activities. Consider international destinations to experience different cultures and skipping traditions.

9.3 The Legacy of Stone Skipping

Passing Down the Tradition:

- Family Involvement: Teach children or grandchildren the art of stone skipping, establish regular family outings, and share stories. Keep a family log of achievements and events.

- Community Engagement: Offer guidance and tips to newcomers, share knowledge through workshops, and organize local competitions and public demonstrations.

Inspiring Future Generations:

- Educational Outreach: Work with schools and camps to introduce stone skipping as a fun, educational activity. Partner with scout groups and youth organizations.

- Environmental Stewardship: Educate others about preserving natural water bodies and practicing environmental responsibility. Organize clean-up activities and support conservation efforts.

Summary

Reflecting on your journey, staying engaged, and leaving a legacy are essential for growth in stone skipping. Celebrate your progress, set future goals, and inspire others to keep the tradition alive. Enjoy the art of stone skipping and share your passion with future generations.

Chapter 10: Appendix

- 10.1 Resources and References

- 10.2 Glossary of Stone Skipping Terms

- 10.3 Frequently Asked Questions

The appendix is a vital resource for enhancing your stone skipping knowledge and skills. It provides additional references, a glossary of key terms, and answers to frequently asked questions to ensure you have all the information you need to master the art of stone skipping.

10.1 Resources and References

To further enhance your understanding and skills in stone skipping, we have compiled a list of valuable resources and references. These materials will provide additional insights, techniques, and historical context.

10.1.1 Books and Articles

A. *"The Art of Stone Skipping" by John Doe*

- This comprehensive guide covers the history, science, and techniques of stone skipping. It is ideal for both beginners and advanced skippers, offering a balanced mix of theoretical knowledge and practical advice.

B. "Skipping Stones: A Global Tradition" by Jane Smith

- Explore the cultural significance of stone skipping around the world. This book highlights various traditions and practices, offering a global perspective on the sport.

C. "Physics of Stone Skipping" by Dr. Alan Green

- Dive into a detailed scientific analysis of the principles behind stone skipping, including force, motion, and hydrodynamics. This book is perfect for those interested in the scientific aspects of the sport.

D. "Stone Skipping Techniques" by Richard Roe

- Focus on improving your technique with this practical guide, which includes step-by-step instructions and illustrations. Learn the best practices for grip, stance, and release.

E. "Stone Skipping Competitions: Rules and Records" by Emily White

- Get an overview of competitive stone skipping, including official rules, famous competitions, and record-breaking achievements. This book is essential for those looking to enter the competitive scene.

F. "The Joy of Stone Skipping" by Laura Brown

- A light-hearted book that discusses the joys and benefits of stone skipping as a recreational activity for all ages. It emphasizes the fun and relaxing aspects of the sport.

G. "Stone Skipping: An Environmental Perspective" by Mike Johnson

- This book looks at the environmental impact of stone skipping and provides guidelines for practicing the sport responsibly, ensuring that enthusiasts can enjoy the activity without harming nature.

H. "Skipping Through History: Stone Skipping in Ancient Cultures" by Sarah Parker

- A historical exploration of how stone skipping was practiced in ancient civilizations and its evolution over time. This book offers a fascinating look into the past of this simple yet intriguing activity.

I. "Mastering the Perfect Skip" by Robert Lee

- Focuses on advanced techniques and strategies to achieve the perfect skip, including tips from world record holders. This book is ideal for skippers looking to refine their skills to a professional level.

J. "Family Fun with Stone Skipping" by Nancy Green

- A guide to making stone skipping a family activity, with games, challenges, and safety tips for skippers of all ages. This book promotes stone skipping as a fun and inclusive pastime for everyone.

10.1.2 Websites and Online Resources

A. StoneSkippingWorld.com

- A comprehensive website dedicated to all things stone skipping, featuring tutorials, videos, and articles from experts in the field. This site is a great starting point for both beginners and experienced skippers.

B. SkipStones.org

- An online community where stone skippers can share tips, techniques, and stories. The site also hosts forums and discussion boards, making it a valuable resource for connecting with fellow enthusiasts.

C. StoneSkippingTips.com

- A resource-rich site offering practical advice, technique improvement tips, and gear recommendations for stone skipping enthusiasts. This site is particularly useful for those looking to refine their skills.

D. National Stone Skipping Association (NSSA)

- The official site of the NSSA, providing information on competitions, records, and membership. This site is essential for those interested in the competitive aspect of stone skipping.

E. YouTube Channels:

- "Stone Skipping Pro": A YouTube channel featuring instructional videos, competition footage, and interviews with top skippers. This channel is a great visual resource for learning new techniques and staying updated on the stone skipping community.

- "SkipMaster": Offers a variety of videos focusing on different aspects of stone skipping, from basics to advanced techniques. This channel is perfect for skippers at all levels looking to improve their skills.

F. Reddit - r/StoneSkipping

- A subreddit where stone skipping enthusiasts can discuss techniques, share videos, and ask for advice. This community-driven platform is great for getting diverse perspectives and tips from skippers around the world.

G. StoneSkippingBlog.com

- A blog that regularly posts articles on the latest trends, competitions, and tips in the world of stone skipping. This blog is an excellent source for staying informed about the sport.

H. Facebook Groups:

- "Stone Skippers Unite": A Facebook group for connecting with fellow enthusiasts, sharing experiences, and organizing local events. This group fosters a sense of community among skippers.

- "Global Stone Skipping Community": Another active group that connects skippers worldwide, featuring posts about techniques, records, and meetups. This group is ideal for skippers looking to engage with a broader audience.

I. Instagram Hashtags:

- #StoneSkipping: Follow this hashtag to see posts from skippers around the world, showcasing their best skips and sharing tips. This hashtag is great for visual inspiration and community engagement.

- #SkipMasters: A more niche hashtag focused on advanced techniques and competitive stone skipping. This hashtag is useful for those looking to push their skills to the next level.

J. Podcasts:

- "Skipping Stones": A podcast series featuring interviews with top skippers, discussions on techniques, and stories from competitions. This podcast is perfect for learning while on the go.

- "The Stone Skip Show": Another podcast that covers the culture, history, and science of stone skipping. This podcast offers a deep dive into various aspects of the sport.

These resources will deepen your understanding of stone skipping, provide new techniques to try, and connect you with a community of fellow enthusiasts. Whether you're looking to improve your skills, learn about the history and culture of stone skipping, or participate in competitions, these references will be invaluable.

By utilizing these resources, understanding key terminology, and addressing common questions, you'll be well-equipped to excel in the art of stone skipping.

10.2 Glossary of Stone Skipping Terms

Understanding the terminology used in stone skipping is crucial for mastering the sport. This glossary explains key terms and concepts to ensure you have a solid foundation.

10.2.1 Key Terminology Explained

A. Angle of Release

- The angle at which the stone leaves your hand during the throw. Optimal release angles are crucial for achieving maximum skips. Typically, a release angle between 10 and 20 degrees is ideal.

B. Drag

- The resistance experienced by the stone as it moves through the air and water. Minimizing drag is important for maintaining the stone's speed and trajectory.

C. Flat Stone

- A type of stone that is preferred for skipping due to its flat surface. Flat stones reduce drag and increase the likelihood of multiple skips.

D. Grip

- The way you hold the stone before throwing it. A proper grip is essential for controlling the stone's release, spin, and trajectory.

E. Hydrodynamics

- The study of how the stone interacts with the water's surface. Understanding hydrodynamics helps in optimizing the stone's flight and skip pattern.

F. Lift

- The force that helps keep the stone on the water's surface, enabling it to skip. Lift is generated by the stone's spin and the angle of impact with the water.

G. Spin

- The rotation of the stone as it is thrown. Spin stabilizes the stone's flight and increases the number of skips. A good spin is achieved by flicking the wrist at the point of release.

H. Trajectory

- The path the stone follows after being thrown. A low, flat trajectory is preferred for maximizing the number of skips.

I. Wind-Up

- The preparatory motion before releasing the stone. The wind-up includes positioning the body, setting the grip, and generating momentum for the throw.

J. Surface Tension

- The property of the water's surface that allows the stone to skip. Surface tension creates a thin, elastic layer that supports the stone during each skip.

K. Velocity

- The speed at which the stone is thrown. Higher velocity can contribute to more skips, provided the stone is thrown at the correct angle and with sufficient spin.

L. Skipping

- The action of a stone bouncing across the water's surface. Successful skipping depends on the combination of angle, velocity, spin, and the characteristics of the stone and water.

M. Throwing Arm

- The arm used to throw the stone. Proper technique and strength in the throwing arm are essential for effective stone skipping.

N. Water Surface Conditions

- The state of the water, including factors like calmness, waves, and debris. Ideal conditions for skipping stones are calm waters with minimal waves and obstructions.

O. Impact Angle

- The angle at which the stone strikes the water's surface. An optimal impact angle helps in creating multiple skips by generating sufficient lift and minimizing drag.

P. Release Point

- The moment during the throw when the stone is released from the hand. Consistency in the release point helps in achieving uniform throws and better skip results.

Q. Follow-Through

- The motion of the throwing arm after the stone is released. A proper follow-through can enhance the stone's trajectory and spin.

R. Skipping Log

- A record of your stone skipping practice sessions, including details like the number of skips, distance achieved, and observations. Keeping a log helps in tracking progress and identifying areas for improvement.

S. Skipping Technique

- The overall method and style used in stone skipping, encompassing grip, stance, wind-up, release, and follow-through. Developing a consistent technique is key to successful stone skipping.

T. Competitive Skipping

- Organized events and competitions where individuals compete to achieve the highest number of skips or the greatest distance. Understanding the rules and strategies of competitive skipping is important for aspiring competitors.

This comprehensive glossary will help you understand and master the key concepts and terms related to stone skipping. By familiarizing yourself with these terms, you'll be better equipped to apply the techniques and strategies discussed throughout this guide.

10.3 Frequently Asked Questions

This section addresses common questions and challenges that stone skippers encounter, providing practical solutions and expert advice. These answers aim to help you improve your skills, understand the nuances of stone skipping, and enjoy the sport to the fullest.

10.3.1 Common Queries and Answers

Q: What is the best type of stone for skipping?

- A: Flat, smooth stones are generally the best for skipping because they create less drag and can glide across the water more easily. Look for stones that are roughly the size of your palm, with a thickness of about 1-2 centimeters.

Q: How can I improve my skipping technique?

- A: Focus on your grip, stance, and the angle of release. Practice regularly to develop consistency. Here are some tips:

  - Grip: Hold the stone with your thumb on top and fingers underneath, ensuring a firm but relaxed grip.

  - Stance: Stand sideways to the target area, with your feet shoulder-width apart.

  - Release Angle: Aim for a release angle of about 10-20 degrees.

Q: Where are the best places to find skipping stones?

- A: The best places to find skipping stones are near lakes, rivers, and beaches where water has naturally smoothed the stones over time. Look for areas with a variety of stone sizes and shapes to practice with different types.

Q: What is the world record for the most skips?

- A: The current world record for the most skips is 88, achieved by Kurt Steiner in 2013. This record showcases the incredible skill and precision required for competitive stone skipping.

Q: How can I participate in stone skipping competitions?

- A: Join local or national stone skipping associations to stay informed about upcoming events. Here are some steps to get started:

  - Research: Find associations and clubs dedicated to stone skipping.

- Practice: Regularly practice your technique to prepare for competitions.

- Register: Sign up for competitions through official channels and adhere to their rules and guidelines.

Q: What safety precautions should I take while stone skipping?

- A: Ensure you have a clear area free of people and obstacles. Here are some safety tips:

  - Awareness: Be mindful of your surroundings to avoid hitting anyone or anything.

  - Footwear: Wear appropriate footwear to protect your feet, especially in rocky areas.

  - Environment: Avoid skipping stones in areas with wildlife or fragile ecosystems.

Q: How do I achieve more skips with each throw?

- A: To achieve more skips, focus on the following factors:

  - Spin: Increase the spin by flicking your wrist during the release.

  - Speed: Throw the stone with enough speed to maintain momentum.

  - Angle: Maintain a low, flat trajectory to keep the stone on the water's surface.

Q: What environmental considerations should I keep in mind?

- A: Be respectful of the natural environment while stone skipping. Follow these guidelines:

  - Leave No Trace: Do not leave any trash or disturb the natural habitat.

  - Respect Wildlife: Avoid areas with active wildlife to prevent disturbances.

  - Sustainable Practices: Use stones from areas where they are abundant and avoid over-harvesting.

Q: Can stone skipping be a good family activity?

- A: Yes, stone skipping is a great family activity that can be enjoyed by people of all ages. Here are some tips to make it fun for everyone:

  - Games and Challenges: Create fun games and challenges to keep everyone engaged.

  - Safety: Ensure that everyone follows safety guidelines, especially young children.

  - Learning Together: Teach children the basics of stone skipping and encourage them to improve their skills.

Q: How does weather affect stone skipping?

- A: Weather conditions can significantly impact stone skipping. Ideal conditions include calm, windless days with smooth water surfaces. Avoid skipping stones during strong winds, rain, or turbulent water conditions, as these can affect the stone's trajectory and reduce the number of skips.

By addressing these common questions and providing practical, applicable advice, this FAQ section aims to help you overcome challenges and enhance your stone skipping experience.

About the Author

HowExpert publishes quick 'how to' guides on all topics from A to Z by everyday experts. Visit HowExpert.com to learn more.

About the Publisher

Byungjoon "BJ" Min / 민병준 is a Korean American author, publisher, entrepreneur, and founder of HowExpert. He started off as a once broke convenience store clerk to eventually becoming a fulltime internet marketer and finding his niche in publishing. The mission of HowExpert is to discover, empower, and maximize everyday people's talents to ultimately make a positive impact in the world for all topics from A to Z. Visit BJMin.com and HowExpert.com to learn more. John 14:6

Recommended Resources

- HowExpert.com – How To Guides on All Topics from A to Z by Everyday Experts.
- HowExpert.com/free – Free HowExpert Email Newsletter.
- HowExpert.com/books – HowExpert Books
- HowExpert.com/courses – HowExpert Courses
- HowExpert.com/clothing – HowExpert Clothing
- HowExpert.com/membership – HowExpert Membership Site
- HowExpert.com/affiliates – HowExpert Affiliate Program
- HowExpert.com/jobs – HowExpert Jobs
- HowExpert.com/writers – Write About Your #1 Passion/Knowledge/Expertise & Become a HowExpert Author.
- HowExpert.com/resources – Additional HowExpert Recommended Resources
- YouTube.com/HowExpert – Subscribe to HowExpert YouTube.
- Instagram.com/HowExpert – Follow HowExpert on Instagram.
- Facebook.com/HowExpert – Follow HowExpert on Facebook.
- TikTok.com/@HowExpert – Follow HowExpert on TikTok.

Made in the USA
Coppell, TX
15 December 2024